The Very Best Recipes From The Perfect Pantry®

By
Lydia Walshin

ISBN 978-0-9897011-5-0

All of the text and photographs in this book previously appeared on my blog, The Perfect Pantry (www.theperfectpantry.com). Slight edits in format have been made from the original blog posts to fit the book's page size.

About this book

Over the past ten years, many readers of my food blog, The Perfect Pantry, have written to tell me which recipes from my kitchen have become their favorites. I love hearing from all of you, especially when you've changed one of my recipes to make it your own. Recipes, after all, are only a starting point.

Now I'm happy to share the recipes that are *my* favorites. It's a quirky selection, far more savory than sweet, from cuisines all around the globe. It wasn't easy to choose 82 recipes out of more than 2,500, but in the end, the recipes here are those my family enjoys and that I turn to again and again when entertaining or in need of outstanding, and easy, comfort food.

The recipes in this book appear **alphabetically**, using the same titles on the blog. Remember that there are hundreds more recipes on The Perfect Pantry; the recipe index on the blog will help you discover them.

For the sake of space in this book, I've left all of the "head notes" – the stories behind the recipes – on the blog itself. Please use the search box at the top of the blog page (www.theperfectpantry.com) to find each recipe, where you'll learn more about the backstories and the ingredients, plus some tips and techniques.

Note: some favorite recipes that appear in my ebooks are not featured here. You can preview the ebooks on Amazon.com (plus some special added recipes and videos): www.amazon.com/author/lydiawalshin.

As I always say, *you* are the most important ingredient in The Perfect Pantry. I'm grateful beyond measure for your support and enthusiasm. Keep your pantry stocked, and I hope you enjoy this book!

With many thanks,
Lydia

Albornia de chayote {vegetarian}

Serves 6.

Scrambled eggs with Caribbean flair.

Ingredients

2 green chayote squash*, quartered, pith removed, and diced (do not peel)
1/2 tsp olive oil
2 Tbsp sofrito (store-bought or homemade)
1/2 green pepper, diced
1/2 red pepper, diced
1/2 yellow pepper, diced
1 onion, diced
7 eggs

Directions

Bring 2 cups of water to the boil in a saucepan. Add the chayote, and boil uncovered for 30 minutes until the chayote is cooked through. Drain and set aside.
In a large frying pan, heat the olive oil and sofrito, and stir in peppers and onion. Sauté, stirring often, 3-4 minutes over medium-high heat. Add the chayote, and cook 1 minute. Reduce heat to low.

In a large bowl, beat the eggs and stir into the vegetable mixture. Stir constantly until the eggs are cooked, approximately 4-5 minutes.

* Chayote, also known as mirliton, is a pale green, almost pear-shaped squash, with a dimple on the bottom. If you can't find it, you can substitute a firm zucchini or yellow (summer) squash.

Apple spice bread

Ever so slightly adapted from the *New York Times Bread & Soup Cookbook*. Makes 1 loaf.

The perfect snack with afternoon tea.

Ingredients

2 cups all-purpose unbleached flour
1 tsp baking soda
1 tsp kosher salt
1/2 tsp nutmeg
1 tsp cinnamon
1/4 tsp ground cloves
1/4 cup whole wheat flour
1/2 cup vegetable shortening
3/4 cup light brown sugar
2 eggs
1 tsp pure vanilla extract
1 cup grated tart apples (Granny Smith, Macoun, or a mix -- approx. 3 large apples)
1/2 cup buttermilk (made from powdered buttermilk, or fresh)

Directions

Preheat the oven to 350°F. Spray a loaf pan with baking spray. Sift together first 6 ingredients. Stir in whole wheat flour. Set aside.

In a large bowl, or stand mixer, cream the shortening and sugar. Add vanilla and eggs, and stir to combine. Then, alternating a little bit at a time, add dry ingredients, buttermilk and apples to the egg mixture. Pour the batter into the prepared loaf pan. Bake for 1 hour, until a skewer inserted into the thickest part comes out clean.

Let cool in the pan for 15 minutes, then turn out onto a rack and let cool to desired serving temperature. Serve slightly warm with fresh whipped cream or vanilla ice cream, or serve cold. (Can be frozen.)

Asparagus wonton wraps with hoisin, wasabi or mustard filling {vegetarian}

Makes 24.

Let your guests help roll these wonton wraps.

Ingredients

12 medium-thick asparagus spears, bottom woody ends trimmed
3 cups canola oil, for deep frying
48 square wonton skins
2-3 Tbsp (or more as needed) of your filling of choice: hoisin sauce, wasabi mayonnaise, Dijon or hot Chinese mustard
Small bowl of water (1/2 cup)

Directions

Cut each asparagus spear in half crosswise.

In a deep pot, heat the oil over medium heat.

While the oil is heating, form the wonton wraps: Place two wonton skins on a work surface, keeping remaining skins covered with a damp cloth to prevent drying out. Lightly dab the center of one skin with a small drop of filling. Wet the tip of your finger, and run it around the edge of the wonton. Place the second skin on top, and press down lightly to spread the filling and seal the two wontons together.

Place one piece of asparagus diagonally across one corner of the wonton skin "sandwich". Roll the wonton around the asparagus, allowing one end to protrude. Just before you get to the end, dab some water on the wonton to seal it when you finish the roll. Repeat with remaining wonton skins, filling, and asparagus.

Test the oil by standing a bamboo chopstick upright in the pot. If small bubbles appear at the base of the chopstick, the oil is hot enough. Using a wire mesh skimmer or slotted spoon, lower 5 or 6 wontons into the pot. Fry until golden, about 2-3 minutes. Remove to a plate covered with paper towels to drain. Repeat with remaining wonton wraps.

Serve hot.

Avocado and edamame spread on toast {vegan}

Makes 1 cup; can be multiplied.

Nobody will guess what's in this spread!

Ingredients

1 ripe avocado
1 cup edamame (soy beans), defrosted if frozen, cooked and drained
1 Tbsp sesame oil
1 Tbsp rice vinegar
Juice of 1 lime
1/4 tsp kosher salt
2-3 drops of Sriracha, or more to taste
Toasted slices of bread (or crackers)
1 Tbsp sesame seeds, white or black

Directions

Place the avocado and cooked edamame in the work bowl of a food processor fitted with a metal blade. Pulse until finely chopped. Add sesame oil, rice vinegar, lime juice, salt and Sriracha, and process until the mixture is a creamy texture.

Heat a small nonstick frying pan, and toast the sesame seeds in the dry pan, shaking the pan occasionally, until they are just fragrant, 2-3 minutes.

Spread the avocado mixture on toasted bread or crackers. Sprinkle with sesame seeds.

Baby kale and cabbage salad with feta, olives, and Greek dressing {vegetarian, gluten-free}

Serves 2 as a main course, 4 as a side salad.

A robust main course salad.

Ingredients

FOR THE DRESSING:
2 Tbsp plain low-fat Greek yogurt
1 Tbsp mayonnaise
1 Tbsp powdered buttermilk + 1/2 cup water (use 1/4 cup water for a thick dressing)
1 tsp Dijon mustard
1/2 tsp Greek seasoning
1 heaping tsp grated Parmigiano-Reggiano cheese
Fresh black pepper, to taste

FOR THE SALAD:
4 cups mixed baby kale and shredded cabbage
18 pitted kalamata olives, sliced in half lengthwise
18 cherry tomatoes, sliced in half lengthwise
4 hard-boiled eggs, quartered lengthwise
1/2 cup feta cheese, crumble

Directions

Whisk together all of the dressing ingredients in a large mixing bowl.

Add the salad ingredients to the dressing, and toss gently to combine.

Serve at room temperature.

Bacon and egg tartine

Serves 2; can be multiplied.

A real wow for a fancy brunch.

Ingredients

2 slices of rustic or sourdough bread
1 tsp olive oil
4-6 slices of center-cut bacon
A large handful of mixed salad greens
1 hard-boiled egg, sliced

FOR THE VINAIGRETTE:
1 Tbsp Dijon mustard
1-1/2 tsp agave nectar
3 Tbsp balsamic vinegar
3 Tbsp extra virgin olive oil
1/4 tsp kosher salt
1/4 tsp black pepper

Directions

Heat an electric panini press to high/sear, or heat a ridged grill pan on the stove top. Paint one side of each slice of bread with olive oil, and set oiled side down on a plate.

Top the dry side of the bread with 2-3 slices of bacon, in a single layer. Place the bread into the panini press, and close the press. Cook for 2-3 minutes, until the bacon is cooked but not overly crisp.

Place the vinaigrette ingredients in a small jar with a tight-fitting lid, and shake the jar until the dressing is emulsified (thickened).

In a small bowl, toss the salad greens with just enough vinaigrette to moisten them. (You can save extra vinaigrette in the jar in the refrigerator.)

Set half of the greens on each slice of bread. Arrange slices of egg on top, and season lightly with salt and pepper. Serve immediately.

Baked stuffed shrimp

Serves 4, can be doubled and more.

A holiday classic from my friends Bob and Charlotte.

Ingredients

1 stalk celery, diced
1-2 large cloves of garlic, minced
1 Tbsp butter
60 Ritz crackers
1 stick (8 Tbsp) butter, melted (easiest in a microwave for 45 seconds)
Juice of 1 lemon
1 Tbsp chopped flat-leaf parsley
2-3 Tbsp white wine
Lots of black pepper, to taste
20 jumbo shrimp (U-12 size)
Paprika, for garnish

Directions

Preheat the oven to 375°F.

In a small frying pan, heat 1 Tbsp of butter. Sauté the celery and garlic for 3-4 minutes on low heat, until softened but not browned. Add to a large mixing bowl.

Crush the crackers with your hands so the crumbs are quite coarse, and add to the bowl with the celery. Stir in the melted butter, lemon juice, parsley, white wine and pepper. The mixture should be fairly dry but should just hold together. Taste, and add, as needed, more lemon juice, more pepper, or more wine. The crackers are salty, so you won't need salt.

To prepare the shrimp: remove the shell, leaving the tail section on. Turn the shrimp with the inside of the curve facing up. Butterfly the shrimp by running a sharp paring knife along the length of the inside, cutting down but not all the way through. You should be able to flatten the shrimp, except for the tail section, and scrape out any black vein.

Set one shrimp on a plate, cut side facing up (the tail should be standing up, too). Mound one tablespoon of cracker filling on the shrimp, and smooth into a large mound. Place the shrimp on a baking sheet lined with a Silpat (silicone liner) or sprayed with nonstick spray. Repeat until all of the shrimp are stuffed. Sprinkle each shrimp with a tiny bit of paprika.

Bake for 20 minutes or until the shrimp are cooked and the stuffing is browned on top.

Serve warm or at room temperature.

Black bean and peach soup {vegan, gluten-free}

Serves 6.

Fruit lightens up this black bean soup.

Ingredients

2 tsp canola oil
1 large onion, chopped
2 cloves garlic, minced
2 plum tomatoes, chopped*
1-1/2 tsp cumin
Pinch of red pepper flakes (optional)
1 lb *cooked* dry black beans, or 3 15-oz cans black beans, rinsed and drained
1 qt chicken stock
2 Tbsp mild barbecue sauce, any type
8-16 oz peach salsa* (to taste: I use 8 oz of my friend Lucia's homemade, or 16 oz of Newman's Own Peach Salsa)
1 large ripe peach, peeled and chopped
Kosher salt and fresh ground black pepper, to taste

Directions

In a 6-quart stockpot, heat the oil over medium heat. Add the onion, and cook for 2-3 minutes, until translucent. Add garlic and tomatoes, stir, and cook for 2 minutes. Stir in the cumin, and continue to cook for 1 minute. Add beans, chicken stock, barbecue sauce and salsa. Bring to a boil, then reduce to low heat and cook, partially covered, for 20 minutes, stirring occasionally to keep the beans from sticking to the bottom of the pot.

Add the fresh peach, and cook for another 10 minutes. With a wooden spoon, mash some of the beans against the side of the pot; this will help thicken the soup, as will the pectin in the fruit. Cook for 10 more minutes, stirring now and then, until soup reaches desired thickness. Taste, and season as needed with salt and pepper.

*Note: if you use a tomato-based peach salsa, eliminate the plum tomato in this recipe.

Broccoli eggrolls

Makes approximately 75 eggrolls.

Always a hit, with a bowl of "duck" sauce.

Ingredients

1 small onion, diced
1 lb boneless chicken breast, diced (optional; you can substitute tofu)
1 small bunch broccoli, chopped, stems peeled and diced
1/4 lb mushrooms, chopped
Mung beans or alfalfa sprouts -- a large handful
2 Tbsp oyster-flavored sauce
3 Tbsp reduced-sodium soy sauce
1 tsp sesame oil
1/2 package sugar substitute, or 1 tsp sugar
2 packages eggroll wrappers
Peanut oil for frying (1 whole bottle)
Plum sauce (a.k.a. duck sauce) or hoisin sauce, for dipping

Directions

TO MAKE THE FILLING: In a nonstick frying pan or wok over medium-high heat, saute onion in 2 Tbsp peanut oil for 2 minutes. Add chicken, and cook for 3 minutes, turning constantly. Add broccoli, mushrooms and bean sprouts, and cook 5 minutes. In a small bowl mix oyster sauce, soy sauce, sesame oil and sugar substitute, and add to broccoli mixture. Cook for 2 more minutes, stirring constantly, and set aside to cool for 10 minutes or more.

Fill wok half way with remaining peanut oil (or if you have a deep-frying contraption, use that), and heat to a medium-high temperature. While the oil is heating, begin to fill the eggroll wrappers.

Place 1-2 tsp of filling in the lower third of a wrapper, fold the bottom up over the mixture, then fold the sides in and roll the wrapper. Seal with a dab of water. (Folding directions are on the back of the eggroll wrapper package.)

Fry 3 or 4 at a time for 2 minutes, or until golden brown. Drain on paper towels. Serve with plum sauce.

Broccoli, mushroom, egg and cheese breakfast casserole {vegetarian, gluten-free}

Serves 5-6.

One of a dozen egg casseroles on the blog.

Ingredients

1 medium onion, diced
2 cups roughly chopped broccoli florets
1/2 cup roughly chopped mushrooms (any variety; I like cremini)
8 large eggs
2 Tbsp nonfat milk
7 oz shredded cheese (I use fat-free mozzarella)
1 Tbsp dried thyme leaf, or 2 Tbsp fresh thyme leaves
1/4 tsp kosher salt
1/2 tsp fresh black pepper
Cooking spray

Directions

Preheat the oven to 375°F.

Place the onion, broccoli and mushrooms in a microwave-safe glass bowl (I use a 4-cup glass measuring cup). Add 1 tablespoon of water. Cover with plastic wrap, and be sure to leave a small vent hole. Microwave on high for 2 minutes. If the broccoli hasn't softened, cook on high for another minute. Uncover, drain off any liquid, and set aside.

Spray a casserole dish with cooking spray. Spread the vegetables in the dish, and allow them to cool slightly while you prepare the remaining ingredients.

In a large bowl, whisk the eggs until slightly frothy. Add the milk, and whisk to combine. With a rubber spatula, stir in the shredded cheese, thyme, salt and pepper. Pour the egg mixture over the vegetables in the casserole dish. Draw the spatula through the mixture to bring some of the vegetables to the surface.

Bake, uncovered, for 35 minutes, until the eggs are puffy. Serve hot, warm or cold.

Broccoli slaw salad with peanut-mango-Sriracha dressing

Serves 4-6; makes enough dressing for 2 batches.

Sriracha makes everything better!

Ingredients

12 oz bag broccoli slaw, rinsed and dried
1/3 cup peanut butter
Juice of 2 limes
1/4 cup mango nectar
2-3 Tbsp Sriracha, or more, to taste
2 cloves garlic, minced
2 Tbsp fish sauce
2 Tbsp mirin
1-2 Tbsp agave nectar, to taste

Directions

Rinse and dry the broccoli slaw in a salad spinner. Or, if you're making your own slaw, shred 12 ounces of vegetables, and place in a bowl.

In a large mixing bowl, whisk together the remaining ingredients, until the peanut butter is smooth and everything is well incorporated. Taste, and adjust with more lime, mango nectar, Sriracha, fish sauce or agave, to your preference.

Combine as much dressing as you need with the broccoli slaw, and refrigerate for an hour, or several hours, to allow the flavors to come together, and to slightly tenderize the broccoli.

Serve at room temperature.

Brussels and broccoli with maple mustard vinaigrette {vegan, gluten-free}

Serves 4-6.

One of our favorite Thanksgiving side dishes.

Ingredients

4 cups shaved or thinly sliced Brussels sprouts (cut out the root ends before you slice)
4 cups thinly sliced broccoli florets
2 Tbsp extra virgin olive oil
Kosher salt and fresh black pepper

FOR THE VINAIGRETTE:
2 Tbsp maple syrup
2 Tbsp Dijon mustard
2 Tbsp balsamic vinegar
1 garlic clove, minced (or use 1/2 tsp garlic paste from a jar)
Large pinch of black pepper
6 Tbsp extra virgin olive oil

Directions

Preheat oven to 425°F. Line a rimmed baking sheet with aluminum foil.

Spread the Brussels sprouts and broccoli on the baking sheet. Sprinkle on the olive oil, plus a pinch of salt and pepper. Toss with your hands until the vegetables are evenly coated with the oil and seasonings, and spread into a single layer on the baking sheet.

Roast for 12 minutes, until the vegetables are just beginning to show bits of browning on the edges. Remove the pan from the oven.

While the vegetables are cooking, add the vinaigrette ingredients to a jar with a tight fitting lid. Shake vigorously, to emulsify the dressing.

Transfer the warm vegetables to a mixing bowl, and add only as much dressing as you need to moisten them without drowning them. Serve warm, at room temperature, or cold.

Bun gao (rice noodle salad with chicken)

Serves 6 or more, depending on what else you serve.

My favorite Vietnamese noodles for a hot day.

Ingredients

1-1/2 lb rice vermicelli
1 package banh trang (rice paper rounds)
Leftover cooked chicken (1 lb for 6-8 people)
1 dozen cooked and cooled medium shrimp, optional
Shredded carrots
Shredded cucumber (European seedless cukes work best)
Shredded iceberg lettuce (3/4 head for 6 people)
Handful of mint leaves
Mung bean sprouts (1/2 lb for 6 people)
Chopped peanuts (dry roasted, unsalted), for topping – a few tablespoons
Nuoc Cham (recipe on the blog)
Chinese peanut dressing (recipe on the blog)

Directions

Fill a bowl with hot water. Soak the rice vermicelli for 15 minutes, until flexible. Drain.

Bring a large pot of water to a boil. Drop in the rice vermicelli, and cook for 1 minute. Drain, rinse under cold water, and drain again. Set aside.

To make the bun gao salad: To a large serving bowl, add the cooked rice vermicelli, carrots, cucumber, lettuce, bean sprouts, and mint leaves.

Top with chicken. Toss with nuoc cham. Top with chopped peanuts and serve at room temperature or cool.

(If assembling the salad ahead, don't add the dressing until you are ready to serve.).

Butternut squash, peanut and chipotle soup {gluten-free}

Serves 4-6.

So creamy, without a drop of cream.

Ingredients

2 tsp olive oil
1 red onion, peeled and cut into chunks
1-1/4 lb cubed peeled butternut squash
1 chipotle pepper in adobo, diced, plus 1-2 tsp adobo sauce (to taste)
2 garlic cloves, roughly chopped
2 tsp ground cumin
2 Tbsp peanut butter
3 cups chicken stock (homemade or low-sodium store-bought)
1 Tbsp honey or agave nectar, or more, to taste
Black pepper, to taste

Directions

In a Dutch oven or heavy stock pot, heat the oil over low heat. Add the onion, and sauté, stirring occasionally, for 3 minutes, until quite soft and just beginning to brown.

Stir in the cubed squash, and cook for 3-4 minutes, until the squash starts to brown here and there. Then, stir in the chipotle pepper, garlic and cumin. Stir everything together, and add the peanut butter. Stir again, and cook for 1 minute or until the peanut butter begins to melt.

Pour in the chicken stock, raise the heat to high, and bring the soup to a boil. Then, reduce heat to simmer, cover the pot, and cook for 25 minutes, until the squash is very soft.

Remove the pot from the stove, and purée with an immersion blender (let the soup cool for a few minutes, then blend in a food processor, in batches if necessary). Return the pot to the stove, taste, and season with honey and black pepper. Serve hot. Can be made ahead and frozen.

Canadian breakfast turkey meatballs with maple and bacon

Makes 12-14 large meatballs; serves 6. Meatballs (without the glaze) can be made ahead and frozen.

A special treat for my family up north.

Ingredients

FOR THE MEATBALLS:
1-1/4 lb ground turkey (93% fat-free)
1/2 cup plain nonfat Greek yogurt
1/2 cup panko bread crumbs
1 large egg
1/4 tsp kosher salt
1/2 tsp fresh black pepper
1 tsp maple sugar or maple pepper

FOR THE GLAZE:
4 strips of center-cut bacon
1 cup maple syrup
6 oz + 3 Tbsp nonalcoholic beer, divided
Pinch of kosher salt

Directions

Preheat oven to 425°F. Line a rimmed baking sheet with a Silpat (silicone mat) or parchment paper, and set aside.

In a large mixing bowl, combine all ingredients for the meatballs. Use your very clean hands to mix the ingredients, making sure the seasonings are well distribute. Do not overmix.

Arrange the meatballs on the prepared baking sheet. Bake for 18-20 minutes, until lightly browned.
While the meatballs are making, make the glaze: In a small nonstick frying pan, cook the bacon until it is browned but not over-crisp. Remove from pan and set aside. When it's cool enough to handle, chop the bacon roughly.

In a deep-sided frying pan, wok or sauce pan, combine the maple syrup, 6 ounces of beer, and salt over medium heat. When the mixture begins to boil, stir frequently to keep it from boiling over as the water releases. Keep stirring, and the glaze will turn darker. When it gets to be the color of cappuccino, and has reduced quite a bit, remove it from the heat, and add the chopped bacon.

Immediately the mixture will begin to set (just like making candy). Off the heat, stir in the remaining 3 tablespoons of beer, to loosen the glaze again.

When the meatballs are cooked, set them on a serving dish. Pour the glaze over. Allow the meatballs to sit for 5 minutes; use a spoon to glaze them with the accumulated liquid in the platter.

Serve warm, with a couple of fried eggs.

Cheese, bacon and guacamole panini

Makes 2 large sandwiches; can be multiplied. This recipe makes extra guacamole.

The Green Muenster, inspired by a food truck.

Ingredients

FOR THE GUACAMOLE:
2 avocados, diced and mashed with a fork
1 chopped plum tomato
1 Tbsp fresh lime juice
1 Tbsp chopped cilantro
1 Tbsp chopped scallions
1 clove garlic, minced
1 chopped jalapeño pepper
Salt and pepper to taste

FOR THE PANINI:
4 slices of bread
8 slices of muenster cheese
4 slices *cooked* bacon
1/2 cup guacamole
4 tsp mayonnaise
Olive oil

Directions

In a mixing bowl, smash together all of the guacamole ingredients with a fork, and set aside. You can make this way ahead, and refrigerate until panini time.

Preheat your panini press or griddle.

Assemble the sandwiches: For each sandwich, place a piece of bread on a plate. Slather it with mayonnaise on one side. Top it with 2 slices of cheese, 2 slices of bacon, 1/4 cup of guacamole, and 2 additional slices of cheese. Smear the other slice of bread with mayonnaise, and top the sandwich.

Use a brush to paint the outside of the sandwich, on both sides, with olive oil. Place both sandwiches on your panini press or griddle. Grill for 2-3 minutes, until the cheese just begins to melt.

Serve hot.

Chicken and spaghetti squash casserole with bell peppers, olives and cheese {gluten-free}

Serves 6.

A great casserole for spaghetti squash fans.

Ingredients

1 spaghetti squash, 2- to 2-1/2 lbs
2 tsp extra virgin olive oil
1 lb boneless, skinless chicken breast, cut into 1/2 by 1-inch slices
1 onion, sliced
2 bell peppers, sliced (I like to use different color peppers)
1 large garlic clove, sliced
1 Tbsp dried thyme
1/4 cup medium black olives
1/2 cup dry white wine
1/2 tsp kosher salt
1/2 tsp fresh black pepper
1/4 cup grated Parmigiano-Reggiano or romano cheese
4 oz grated low-fat Italian cheese blend (or mozzarella)
1/4 cup chopped fresh flat-leaf parsley

Directions

Cook the spaghetti squash in a pressure cooker, oven or slow cooker.

PRESSURE COOKER METHOD: Trim off the stem end of the squash, and cut the squash in half lengthwise. With a spoon, scoop out the seeds and stringy bits. Place the two halves in the pressure cooker and add 1 cup of water. Cook on High Pressure for 8 minutes, and use the Quick Release method to release pressure (follow the instructions that came with your pressure cooker). When the pressure valve drops, open the lid. Use tongs to remove the squash halves to a platter, and let them cool while you make the rest of the dish. Then, use a fork to scrape the "spaghetti" out of the skin.

OVEN ROASTING METHOD: Preheat the oven to 375°F. Cut the squash in half lengthwise, and scoop out the seeds. Place the two halves cut side up on a rimmed baking sheet. Drizzle each half with extra virgin olive oil. Bake for 45 minutes, or until the squash is tender when pierced with a knife. Remove from the oven and set aside to cool while you make the rest of the dish; then, use a fork to scrape the "spaghetti" out of the skin.

SLOW COOKER METHOD: You'll need to start this first thing in the morning to have the squash ready for dinner. Wash the whole squash to remove any surface dirt, and prick it all over with a sharp paring knife. Place the whole squash in a 4-quart oval slow cooker. Add 1-1/2 cups of water. Cover and cook on LOW for 6 hours. Remove squash from the cooker (with tongs), and set aside until it's cool enough to cut open. Scoop out the seeds, and then use a fork to scrape the "spaghetti" out of the skin.

Now that your squash is cooked....

If you've used your pressure cooker or slow cooker for the squash, preheat the oven to 375°F. Coat a casserole dish (approximately 9x13) with cooking spray, and set aside.

Heat a large nonstick frying pan over medium heat. Add olive oil, chicken and onion. Sauté for 3-4 minutes, stirring frequently, until the chicken is no longer pink.

Toss in the bell peppers, garlic, thyme and olives. Continue to cook, stirring, for 2-3 minutes, until the peppers are softened slightly. Pour in the wine, salt and pepper. Stir until everything is combined, and cook for 2 minutes, until most of the liquid evaporates. Remove from heat.

Place the "spaghetti" strands in a large mixing bowl, and add the chicken and pepper mixture from the frying pan. Stir in the two cheeses and parsley, until everything is combined. Pour the mixture into the prepared casserole dish.
Cover the casserole with aluminum foil, and bake for 30 minutes. Then, uncover and bake for an additional 10 minutes.

Serve hot. Can be made up to one day ahead and reheated in a 350° oven.

Chicken enchilada roll-ups stuffed with rice and beans {gluten-free}

Serves 8; can be multiplied.

These roll-ups reheat so easily.

Ingredients

Quick and easy black beans and rice (make 1/2 the recipe; recipe in this book and on the blog)
8 boneless, skinless chicken breast halves*
2 cups shredded cheese, Monterey Jack or Cheddar (I like low-fat four-cheese Mexican blend)
13-oz can mild red enchilada sauce (make sure to use gluten-free, if needed)

Directions

Preheat oven to 375°F. Spread a few tablespoons of enchilada sauce in the bottom of a straight-sided 9x13-inch casserole dish, and set aside.

Make the beans and rice (this can be done days ahead of time). Cool to room temperature, or refrigerate.

Trim the chicken breasts of visible fat and tendons. Working with one at a time, place each breast between two large sheets of parchment, wax paper, or plastic wrap. Use a meat mallet, or something else that's heavy (I use my rolling pin or a small frying pan), to pound the breast out to 1/4-inch thick. *If you buy thin-sliced chicken breasts at the market, you can skip this step, but you won't get the therapeutic benefits of pounding the chicken!

In a large bowl, mix together the beans and rice with 1-1/2 cups of the cheese.
Set out all of the flattened chicken breasts on a plate or countertop. Divide the beans and rice mixture evenly. Carefully roll each chicken breast around the filling, and secure it with a toothpick. (It will be messy. Don't worry.) Place the chicken rolls seam

side down in the prepared casserole dish. Continue filling and rolling the chicken breasts until all are done.

Pour the remaining enchilada sauce over all of the chicken, and sprinkle the remaining cheese on top. Cover the pan with aluminum foil.

Bake for 20 minutes. Then uncover the pan, and bake for an additional 15 minutes, or until the chicken is cooked to 160°F when tested with an instant-read thermometer.

Remove the pan from the oven, cover with the aluminum foil, and let sit for 10 minutes (the temperature will come up to 165°F, indicating the chicken is fully cooked).

Serve warm, with a bit of the sauce, or allow to cool completely, and freeze. These can be made way ahead, and pulled out of the refrigerator or freezer a few at a time for easy meals.

Chicken lo mein

Serves 6.

My version just might be better than take-out!

Ingredients

1 lb fresh Chinese egg noodles (or use dry spaghetti)
2 tsp peanut or canola oil
1 lb boneless, skinless chicken breast, cut into bite-size pieces
1 small onion, diced, or 4-5 scallions, chopped
1 clove garlic, peeled, sliced thin
4-oz can sliced mushrooms
1/2 cup Cantonese 3-2-1 sauce (3 parts reduced-sodium soy sauce, 2 parts oyster sauce, 1 part sesame oil), or more as needed
2 cups mung bean sprouts (optional), rinsed under cold water

Directions

Bring 6 quarts of water to a boil; cook egg noodles over high heat until they float to the surface, then reduce heat and cook for 2-3 minutes until al dente (or cook spaghetti according to package directions). Drain, but do not rinse, and reserve the cooking water.

In a large wok or frying pan, heat the oil. Add the chicken and stir fry for 1-2 minutes, until lightly brown all over. Add the onion, and stir for 1-2 minutes, until translucent. Add the garlic and mushrooms, and stir for 1 minute. Add the Cantonese 3-2-1, plus 1-2 tablespoons of the reserved cooking water, and stir for 1 minute until the meat is coated. Add the cooked noodles and bean sprouts, and stir thoroughly for 2-3 minutes, until the ingredients are combined and the sauce is absorbed into the noodles. If needed, add more soy sauce and oyster sauce, to taste.

Serve hot or at room temperature.

Chicken satay {gluten-free}

This simple marinade is adapted from *The Asian Grill*. Serves 6-8.

Just like we ate at roadside stands in Malaysia.

Ingredients

1 cup coconut milk
1 Tbsp granulated sugar
1 tsp ground coriander
1/2 tsp ground turmeric
1/4 tsp ground cumin
1/4 tsp kosher salt
A pinch of fresh ground black pepper
2-3 lbs boneless, skinless chicken breasts, cut against the grain into 1/8-inch-thick slices
12 long bamboo skewers, or other skewers of your choice
Peanut sauce (use your favorite, or find one on the blog)

Directions

In a small bowl, whisk together everything except the chicken, until the ingredients are incorporated and the sugar is dissolved. Stir in the chicken, and transfer all to a ziploc bag. Squeeze out the air, and seal the bag. Massage the chicken until it's coated all around, and refrigerate for 2 hours.

Soak skewers in water for at least 30 minutes.

Meanwhile, heat your grill to high heat, or prepare a stovetop grill pan. Thread 4-6 pieces of chicken on each skewer, keeping the chicken bunched toward the bottom end of the skewer. Grill the chicken, turning frequently, until crisp, 2 minutes per side.

Serve with peanut sauce for dipping.

Chickpea gremolata with green olives, pine nuts and raisins {vegan, gluten-free}

Serves 6 as a side dish, 4 as an entree.

So easy in the pressure cooker or Instant Pot.

Ingredients

1-1/2 cups dried chickpeas
4 cloves garlic, peeled and left whole
1 bay leaf
Pinch of kosher salt
5 Tbsp extra virgin olive oil
Heaping 1/4 cup pine nuts
1-1/2 cups chopped flat-leaf parsley
1 Tbsp dried oregano
1 Tbsp lemon zest
2 Tbsp lemon juice (1-2 lemons, depending on size)
1/2 cup pitted green olives, roughly chopped
Heaping 1/4 cup raisins (gold, brown, or a mix)
1/2 tsp kosher salt
1/4 tsp fresh black pepper

Directions

Rinse the chickpeas under cool water, and pick out any stones. Add the chickpeas to the pressure cooker, along with 6 cups of water, 2 of the garlic cloves, bay leaf, and a large pinch of kosher salt. Drizzle in 1 tablespoon of the olive oil.

Lock the pressure cooker top. Cook at High Pressure for 40 minutes, then use Natural Pressure Release to finish the cooking. When the pressure valve drops, carefully open the pressure cooker. Taste one of the chickpeas; it should be cooked through, but not mushy. If the beans are not quite done, lock the top again and cook at High Pressure for an additional 5 minutes. Quick Release the steam so the chickpeas don't get overcooked. Turn off the cooker.

Drain the chickpeas, and reserve 2 cups of the bean cooking liquid. Discard the bay leaf.
While the chickpeas are cooking, toast the pine nuts. Heat a small nonstick frying pan, and toast the nuts over medium heat, shaking the pan often to keep the nuts from

burning, for 3-4 minutes. The pine nuts should be aromatic and just slightly browned. Remove the pan from heat and set aside.

On a cutting board, roughly chop together the parsley, oregano, olives, remaining 2 garlic cloves, and lemon zest.

Set the pressure cooker to Sauté, and heat the remaining 4 tablespoons of olive oil. Stir in the parsley mixture, and cook, stirring frequently, for 1 minute. Add the chickpeas, lemon juice and raisins, plus the salt and pepper. Pour in 1 cup of the reserved chickpea cooking liquid. Stir everything together and cook for 2-3 minutes, uncovered, until the flavors come together and most of the liquid has been absorbed. Add the toasted pine nuts, and stir gently. Season with more salt and pepper if needed.

Serve hot, warm or chilled.

Chinese "spaghetti and meat sauce"

Serves 3-4.

In our house, this dish is the #1 comfort food.

Ingredients

8 oz fresh egg noodles or dry spaghetti
1 Tbsp peanut or canola oil
1/2 lb ground beef
2 scallions, sliced
1/2 lb cremini mushrooms, sliced
1 tsp chili paste with garlic
2 tsp oyster-flavored sauce
3 tsp reduced-sodium soy sauce
1/4 cup mung bean sprouts (optional)

Directions

Cook fresh noodles or dry spaghetti in a large pot of boiling water, until they are just underdone. Drain and set aside.

Heat a wok or large frying pan over high heat. Add the oil, then the beef, and cook, stirring and breaking up the beef as you go, until the beef is lightly browned. Add scallions and mushrooms, and continue stir-frying until the mushrooms are starting to brown.

Stir in the chili paste, oyster sauce and soy sauce, then add the noodles and stir to combine everything.

Top with bean sprouts, and serve hot.

Cod, bacon, and sweet potato chowder

Serves 3-4; can be multiplied.

Sweet potatoes in chowder? Why not?

Ingredients

4 slices bacon, diced
2 Tbsp butter
1 small sweet potato, peeled and diced
1 stalk celery, diced
2 scallions, white and green parts, thinly sliced
3 Tbsp all-purpose unbleached flour
2 cups chicken stock, low-sodium store-bought or homemade, or clam broth
2 tsp fresh tarragon, chopped
1-1/4 lb cod chunks, any size (large pieces will break up into the chowder)
Kosher salt and fresh black pepper, to taste
3/4 cup half-and-half

Directions

In a Dutch oven or heavy stock pot, cook the bacon over medium heat, until just starting to brown (but not yet crisp). With a slotted spoon, remove the bacon from the pot and set aside.

Add the butter to the pot, and when it melts, stir in the sweet potato, celery and scallions. Sauté, stirring frequently, until the sweet potato is cooked through and just beginning to brown around the edges, 3-5 minutes.

Sprinkle in the flour, and stir to incorporate it with the vegetables and butter. Stir constantly to keep the vegetables from sticking to the pot. When all of the flour is incorporated, pour in the chicken stock. Stir to mix everything together. Raise the heat just a little bit, to bring the stock to a simmer; the stock should begin to thicken slightly.
Reduce the heat to low, and add the tarragon and fish chunks, plus the reserved bacon. Simmer, uncovered, for 3-4 minutes, until the fish is cooked through. If you have large chunks, gently break them up with a wooden spoon.

For the story behind a recipe, and ingredient info, search the recipe name on www.theperfectpantry.com.

When the fish is cooked, taste, and adjust the seasoning with salt and pepper.

Then, stir in the half-and-half. Cook for 2 minutes (do not boil) to make sure everything is well incorporated. The chowder should be nice and thick and coat the back of your spoon.

Serve immediately. Leftover chowder can be refrigerated in an airtight container and served the next day.

Corn chowder with chipotle cream

Serves 4 as a main dish, with salad and bread on the side.

You don't have to eat seafood to love chowder.

Ingredients

1 tsp vegetable or canola oil
1 small onion, peeled and quartered
16 oz frozen organic corn kernels
1 Tbsp fresh thyme leaves (or 1-1/2 tsp dried thyme)
4 cups chicken stock (homemade or low-sodium store-bought), divided
2 chipotle peppers in adobo, minced (or use just one pepper, if you don't want as much heat)
1/2 cup heavy cream
Kosher salt, to taste
Fresh black pepper, to taste

Directions

In a Dutch oven or small heavy stock pot, heat the oil and sauté the onion briefly over medium heat, just until translucent. Add the corn and thyme leaves, stir to combine, and cook for 2 minutes. Then, add 3 cups of the chicken stock. Bring to a boil, then reduce heat to simmer, cover the pot, and cook for 15 minutes.

While the soup is cooking, whisk together the chipotle peppers and cream in a measuring cup, and set aside. (If you don't want all of the fire power of the chipotles, cut down to one pepper, or even just 1 tablespoon of the adobo sauce from the can.)

After the soup has cooked for 15 minutes, remove the pot from heat. Using an immersion blender, pureé the soup to the desired texture, chunky or creamy smooth. If you don't have an immersion blender, allow the soup to cool for 10-15 minutes, then pureé in batches in a stand blender or food processor, and return it to the pot. Return the pot to the stove, and set at lowest heat. Stir in the chipotle cream. If you want a thinner soup, add some or all of the remaining 1 cup of stock. Taste, and add salt and black pepper, to taste (if you use store-bought stock, you might not need any salt). Serve hot. Can be made ahead and refrigerated for up to two days.

Costa Rican gallo pinto (black beans and rice) {vegan, gluten-free}

Serves 4-6 as a side dish.

We ate gallo pinto every day in Costa Rica.

Ingredients

2 cups *cooked* black beans, plus 3/4 cup bean cooking liquid (can be made days in advance)
3 cups *cooked* long-grain white rice, cooled (can be made days in advance)
1 Tbsp vegetable oil
1/2 onion, diced
1 bell pepper, diced (in Costa Rica, this would be a green pepper, but I love the red)
1/2 cup diced celery
2 large cloves garlic, minced
1 tsp dried thyme leaf
1/2 tsp kosher salt, or more to taste
1/2 tsp fresh black pepper, or more to taste
Chopped cilantro for garnish (optional)

Directions

I use a pressure cooker to cook a batch of dry black beans, with no presoaking, in less than an hour (wow!). You can cook beans in a slow cooker or stovetop pot. Make the beans way ahead, even days ahead, and store them in the refrigerator. In a pinch, you can use canned black beans; reserve some of the bean liquid before rinsing the beans.

In a large, deep frying pan, heat the oil over medium heat. Sauté the onion for 2 minutes, until translucent. Add the bell pepper and celery, and continue to cook for 3 minutes. Toss in the garlic and thyme, and stir for 30 seconds.

Gently pour the black beans and reserved 3/4 cup of bean cooking liquid into the pan. Stir well to combine, and try not to break up the beans. Bring the mixture to a simmer. Then, add in the rice, breaking up clumps with your fingers as best you can.

Stir the rice and bean mixture together so that all of the liquid coats the grains of rice, turning them a brownish color.

Season with salt and pepper (this dish needs a lot of salt to be authentically Costa Rican, so don't be afraid to add more than the recipe calls for). Top with chopped fresh cilantro for serving, if you wish.

Couscous salad with chopped vegetables, basil, parsley and pomegranate vinaigrette {vegan}

Serves 2-3; can be multiplied.

A bright and unusual summer salad.

Ingredients

FOR THE POMEGRANATE VINAIGRETTE DRESSING:
2 Tbsp pomegranate vinegar (or use fig vinegar, or red wine vinegar, champagne or balsamic)
1 tsp Dijon mustard
2 Tbsp extra virgin olive oil
Pinch of fresh black pepper

FOR THE SALAD:
2 cups *cooked* Israeli couscous (or use orzo or another leftover cooked small pasta, or use regular couscous)
1 yellow bell pepper, diced
1 small cucumber, diced (I like the small Persian cucumbers)
1 large plum tomato, diced
12 medium black olives, halved
2 large basil leaves, sliced thinly
2-3 tsp chopped fresh parsley

Directions

In a jar with a tight-fitting lid, combine all of the dressing ingredients. Shake the jar vigorously, to emulsify (thicken) the dressing, and set aside.

Toss together all of the salad ingredients in a medium mixing bowl. Drizzle with as much of the salad dressing as you like, and stir gently to combine.

Serve at room temperature, or refrigerate for up to 1 day.

Cuban shrimp in savory sauce {gluten-free}

Serves 6 (with couscous, orzo or rice).

In Cuba, we enjoyed this made with lobster!

Ingredients

3 lbs large shrimp, peeled and deveined
4 Tbsp olive oil
1 large onion, chopped
1 large green pepper, chopped
6 large cloves garlic, minced
1/2 tsp sugar
8 oz tomato sauce
1/4 tsp Tabasco or other hot sauce, or more to taste
3/4 cup dry white wine
2 Tbsp white wine vinegar
1 bay leaf
1/2 cup chopped flat-leaf parsley
Salt and freshly ground black pepper, to taste

Directions

If using frozen shrimp, defrost under cold running water. Fresh shrimp may need to be peeled and deveined.

In a large pan on top of the stove, heat the oil over medium-high heat, and sauté the onions and green pepper for 3 minutes. Add the garlic and cook for 2 minutes. Stir in the remaining ingredients except the shrimp, cover the pot, turn the heat to low, and cook for 20 minutes. Add the shrimp, cover, and cook over low heat for 6-8 minutes until shrimp are just cooked through.

Serve hot.

NOTE: If you have extra sauce, keep it in the fridge for up to 3 days. You can add more shrimp, or diced chicken breast, or scallops, and make a second meal. The sauce will get better and better.

Curried chicken pasta salad with apricots and cashews

Serves 4.

Indian flavors make a really good pasta salad.

Ingredients

FOR THE DRESSING:
1/2 cup mayonnaise
2 Tbsp chutney (I use Major Grey's mango chutney)
1/2 tsp sweet or hot curry powder
1/4 tsp powdered ginger
Pinch of fresh black pepper

FOR THE SALAD:
4 oz mini penne, rotini or other short pasta
2 large boneless, skinless chicken breasts (defrosted, if frozen)
A sprinkling of kosher salt and fresh black pepper
1/4 cup chopped dried apricots
1/4 cup chopped roasted, unsalted cashews
1 Granny Smith apple, diced (do not peel)

Directions

Combine all dressing ingredients in a small mixing bowl. Cover, and refrigerate until ready to use (can be made one day ahead).

Bring 3 quarts of water to a boil in a pot on the stove top. Cook the pasta until al dente (1 minute less than the recommended cooking time on the package). Drain, rinse, and set aside to cool slightly. (Can be made ahead.)

Dry the chicken breasts, and sprinkle with salt and pepper. Grill or broil for approximately 4 minutes per side, or until the inside of the chicken is no longer pink and the pieces are firm to the touch. When cool enough to handle, dice into 1/2-inch pieces. (Can be made ahead.) Place the cooked pasta, diced chicken, apricots, cashews and diced apple in a large mixing bowl. Stir in as much of the dressing as you need (you might not need all of it). Taste, and season with black pepper, if needed. Serve at room temperature or cold. If you're going to serve the salad cold, chill, covered, until ready to serve. Taste again, and adjust seasoning with salt and pepper, if needed.

For the story behind a recipe, and ingredient info, search the recipe name on www.theperfectpantry.com.

Easy Jamaican meat patties

Filling adapted from *Cooking Caribe*. Makes 10-12 meat patties; figure on 1 per person for an appetizer, or 2 per person for lunch.

Inspired by a food cart at the train station!

Ingredients

FOR THE FILLING:
2 Tbsp vegetable oil
1 lb extra lean ground beef
1 medium onion, finely diced
3 garlic cloves, minced
1/4 tsp red pepper flakes (mild or hot; I use mild)
3 scallions, white and green parts, minced
1 Tbsp curry powder
1 Tbsp dried thyme leaf
1/2 tsp ground cumin
Large pinch EACH: kosher salt and fresh black pepper
1/2 cup plain dry bread crumbs
1/2 cup chicken stock (homemade or low-sodium store-bought)

FOR THE PATTIES:
1 package discos, plus 2 additional (12 discos), defrosted
1 egg

Directions

In a medium nonstick frying pan, heat the oil over medium heat. Add the beef, onion, garlic, red pepper flakes and scallions. Stir frequently, breaking up the beef, until the meat is lightly browned (6-7 minutes).

Add the remaining filling ingredients and simmer, stirring often, for 10-15 minutes. The filling will thicken when you add the bread crumbs, but keep stirring and cooking until the filling is moist, but not wet. Remove from heat and set aside to cool for at least 15 minutes.

Preheat oven to 400°F. Line a rimmed baking sheet with a Silpat (silicone mat) or parchment paper, and set aside.

On your countertop, place a small bowl of cool water next to your work area. Set out a large flat plate or platter on which you will form the patties.

Take one disco and set it on the plate. Place a heaping tablespoon of meat filling in the center.

Wet your finger in the water, and run your finger around the entire edge of the disco. Fold the disco over to form a half-moon, and press down on the seam to seal. To strengthen the seal, press into the seam with the tines of a fork. Place the patty on the baking sheet, and continue until all of the patties are formed.

Crack the egg into a small bowl, and beat it with 1 tablespoon of water. Using a pastry brush, paint the tops of the patties with this egg glaze.

Bake 18-20 minutes, until the tops of the patties are lightly browned.

Serve warm. Or, let the patties cool completely, and pack into zip-lock bags to refrigerate or freeze. Reheat in a warm oven before serving.

Egg salad with avocado, jalapeño and lime {vegetarian}

Serves 2-3; can be multiplied.

Kick up your egg salad!

Ingredients

4 hard-boiled eggs, chopped or sliced with an egg slicer
1 small avocado, chopped
1 Tbsp mayonnaise
1 Tbsp roughly chopped fresh flat-leaf parsley
1 tsp minced red bell pepper
1/4 tsp minced jalapeño pepper, or more to taste
Juice of 1/2 lime
1/4 tsp kosher salt
1/4 tsp fresh black pepper

Directions

In a mixing bowl, use a rubber spatula to combine all ingredients, smashing the egg and avocado a little bit here and there.

Taste, and adjust seasoning with more jalapeño, lime, salt or pepper.

Serve chilled or at room temperature, on toast, in a roll-up, or in lettuce leaves.

Granola cookies

Makes 4 dozen.

I've been baking these since my college days.

Ingredients

2 cups unsifted all-purpose unbleached flour
1 tsp baking powder
1 tsp baking soda
1 tsp salt
1 cup shortening
1 cup firmly packed brown sugar
1/2 cup granulated sugar
2 eggs
1 tsp vanilla extract
1-1/2 cups granola (I use Quaker Natural with raisins, but any granola-type cereal will work)
1/2 cup golden raisins, optional (if, like me, you really like raisins)

Directions

Preheat oven to 375°F.

Combine flour, baking powder, baking soda and salt on wax paper, and stir to blend. Cream shortening and sugars together. Add eggs and vanilla, and beat well. Stir in blended dry ingredients, granola and raisins. Mix well.

Refrigerate 30 minutes or until dough is firm enough to handle. Shape dough into 1-inch balls.

Place on ungreased cookie sheet and bake for 10 minutes. Let stand for a minute or two, then transfer to cooling rack.

Greek pasta salad with sun-dried tomato vinaigrette {vegetarian}

Serves 4 as a main course.

The most popular recipe on the blog.

Ingredients

FOR THE DRESSING:
1 garlic clove
7 sun-dried or slow-roasted tomato halves, roughly chopped
2 Tbsp plain nonfat yogurt
1 tsp Greek seasoning
1/4 cup white wine vinegar
1/4 cup extra virgin olive oil
1-1/2 tsp agave nectar (or honey, or sugar substitute)
5-6 tsp water

FOR THE SALAD:
8 oz rotini or other twisty pasta (I use Dreamfields)
1-1/2 cup diced fresh tomatoes, any type
1 cup diced cucumber (I use seedless English cucumber)
1/2 medium green bell pepper, diced
1/2 cup pitted large black olives, sliced in half
3 Tbsp chopped fresh dill
1/2 cup crumbled feta cheese, or more to taste

Directions

In a blender, combine all dressing ingredients, and blend on high speed until smooth. If you'd like the dressing thinner, add a bit more water. Set aside.

Bring 4 quarts of water to the boil in a large pot. Cook the pasta according to package directions; drain and add to a large mixing bowl. Combine all remaining ingredients in the mixing bowl along with as much of the dressing as you like. Garnish with some extra dill fronds, and serve at room temperature.

Greektown turkey meatballs

Makes 36-40 meatballs (or 6 turkey burgers).

We love these meatballs in Greek salads.

Ingredients

1-1/4 lb ground turkey (I use 93% fat-free)
1/2 cup seasoned dry bread crumbs
1/2 cup plain Greek yogurt (I use Fage 0% fat)
1 large egg
1-1/2 Tbsp Greektown Billygoat Seasoning or Penzeys Greek Seasoning (or equivalent mix of dried oregano plus lemon zest, plus one clove of garlic, smashed)
1/2 tsp kosher salt
1/2 tsp fresh black pepper
1 tsp olive oil
1-2 Tbsp flat-leaf parsley, roughly chopped

Directions

Preheat oven to 425°F. Line a rimmed baking sheet with a Silpat (silicone liner), aluminum foil or parchment paper, and set aside.

In a large mixing bowl, combine all ingredients. With your hands, mix until well combined, with the breadcrumbs and yogurt evenly distributed throughout.
Wet your hands with water, and form the turkey mixture into 36-40 meatballs approximately 1-1/4 inches in diameter.

Place on the prepared baking sheet, and bake for 15 minutes, until just slightly brown. Taste one to be sure they're done; the yogurt will keep the meatballs fairly moist.

You can make these ahead, and freeze them. Serve as an appetizer, or add to a Greek salad.

Grilled Asian turkey breast with soy, garlic and chili paste {gluten-free}

Serves 8-10 or more.

A completely different take on turkey.

Ingredients

1 3-4 lb boneless, skinless turkey breast, tenderloins removed (reserve for soup stock)
1/4 cup reduced-sodium soy sauce
2 tsp chili paste with garlic
2 cloves garlic, peeled and sliced
2 scallions, trimmed, cut into large chunks (green and white parts)
1/4 cup water

Directions

Combine all ingredients in a ziploc bag. Seal the bag, pressing out most of the air. Massage the bag to distribute the ingredients evenly, and set in the refrigerator to marinate for at least 6 hours, or (preferably) overnight. Turn the bag over once or twice, if you remember, to marinate the meat more evenly.

When you're ready to cook, remove the turkey from the refrigerator. As it comes to room temperature, preheat your grill on high heat.

Grill the turkey for approximately 10 minutes on each side, until it reaches an internal temperature of 165°F.

Remove the turkey and allow it to sit at room temperature for a few minutes before slicing. Or, cool completely, and refrigerate or freeze.

Grilled peaches with balsamic and granola

Serves 6.

Top with yogurt or vanilla ice cream.

Ingredients

1/2 cup balsamic vinegar
1/4 cup light agave nectar
3 peaches, halved, pits removed (or any stone fruit)
1 Tbsp olive or canola oily
1/2 cup granola (homemade or storebought)

Directions

In a small, deep saucepan, heat the vinegar and agave nectar over medium-high heat until it begins to boil. Continue heating, watching carefully, for 10 minutes or until reduced by 3/4 to a thick (but still pourable) syrup.

Meanwhile, scoop out a bit of the insides of the peach to remove any bits of the pit.

Heat a stove-top grill pan over medium heat. When the pan is hot, brush the cut side of each peach half with olive oil, and place cut side down on the grill pan. Do not move the peaches! Cook for 2 minutes or until nice grill marks appear. Remove peaches from the pan and place cut side up on individual serving plates.

When the syrup is reduced to desired consistency, drizzle it over the peaches.

Top with a bit of granola and serve immediately.

Hawaiian sweet potato salad {vegetarian, gluten-free}

Recipe adapted from *Hurry Up and Wait: Hawaii's Favorite Recipes for the Pressure Cooker and the Slow Cooker.* Serves 4-6.

An unusual spin on potato salad.

Ingredients

3 lbs sweet potatoes, peeled and cut into very large chunks
1/4 tsp grated ginger
1 Tbsp fresh lime juice
1/2 cup plain Greek yogurt (I use nonfat)
1/4 cup mayonnaise
2 tsp Dijon mustard
1 Tbsp sweet curry powder
1/2 tsp agave nectar (optional)
1 cup diced celery
1/2 cup diced red bell pepper
Fresh black pepper, to taste

Directions

Place the potatoes in the pressure cooker with 1 cup of water. Cook on High Pressure for 3 minutes, then Quick Release the pressure. Remove the potatoes from the cooker and set aside to cool while you make the rest of the salad.

In a large mixing bowl, whisk together the ginger, lime juice, yogurt, mayonnaise, mustard and curry powder. Taste the sauce, and add agave nectar if you'd like it a bit sweeter.

Add to the sauce the diced celery and red pepper. Then, gently fold in the slightly cooled sweet potato. Add a pinch of black pepper.

Refrigerate the potato salad for several hours, or overnight, to allow the flavors to meld. Taste again before serving, and add more pepper or some kosher salt, to taste. Serve chilled.

Irish soda bread muffins

Makes 12 muffins.

Fun for Thanksgiving, or for brunch.

Ingredients

Baking spray (PAM with flour, or Baker's Joy)
1-1/2 cups all-purpose unbleached flour
1 cup white whole wheat flour
1-1/2 tsp baking powder
2 tsp baking soda
1 tsp light brown sugar, mixed with 1-1/2 tsp water
1/2 cup golden raisins
1-1/8 cups buttermilk

Directions

Adjust oven rack to center position and preheat to 325°F. Spray a 12-cup muffin tin with baking spray, and set aside.

Place flours, baking powder, baking soda, sugar and raisins in a large bowl and mix well. Add the buttermilk and stir until you have a wet and shaggy dough.

With your hand, knead the dough in the bowl a few times, then empty onto a lightly-floured countertop and knead a bit longer, until the dough comes together in a semi-firm ball. The surface will not be smooth, but that's okay.

Use a sharp knife to cut the dough into 12 equal portions. Roll each into a ball, and place each ball of dough in one of the muffin cups. Make a small slice in the top of each muffin, and let the dough sit on the countertop for 10 minutes.

Bake for 20 minutes, or until the muffins are lightly browned on top, and a toothpick inserted into the center of one comes out clean.

Allow to cool for 3-4 minutes, then serve warm with butter and jam.

Kung pao chicken

Slightly adapted from *Chinese Cooking for Everyone*, an out-of-print cookbook, this recipe serves 4-6.

One of my favorite Chinese take-out dishes.

Ingredients

1-1/4 lb chicken breast, cut into 1/2-inch cubes (defrost if frozen)
3 Tbsp peanut oil
1 tsp Szechuan peppercorns
1 tsp dried red chile pepper, cut into rings
1 tsp shao hsing wine
3 slices ginger root
1 tsp chopped garlic
2 tsp chopped scallion
4 oz roasted unsalted peanuts

FOR THE MARINADE:
1 tsp sugar
1 Tbsp dark soy sauce
1 Tbsp cornstarch

FOR THE SAUCE:
1 tsp sugar
2 tsp distilled white vinegar
1 Tbsp dark soy sauce
3 Tbsp chicken stock
2 tsp cornstarch

Directions

In a small bowl, mix the chicken with the marinade ingredients, and set aside. In a separate bowl, mix all of the sauce ingredients, and set aside. Heat the oil in a wok over high heat, and when the oil is hot, add the peppercorns and chile peppers. When the peppers darken, pour the oil through a strainer into a bowl. Add the chicken, and stir-fry for 1 minute. Then, add the shao hsing wine, ginger, garlic and scallions. Continue to stir, and pour in the sauce (it will be quite thick). Stir for 15 seconds, and add the peanuts. Stir to combine, and serve hot, over rice.

Lamb tagine with garlic, honey and raisins

Serves 4.

So seductively sweet, you'll call it candy.

Ingredients

1-1/2 lb boneless leg of lamb or lamb stew meat, cut into 1-1/2 inch chunks
1 Tbsp Greek seasoning
1 Tbsp lemon zest
1 tsp dried oregano
1 tsp fresh black pepper
2 tsp olive oil
2 cloves garlic, sliced
3/4 cup dry white wine
1/4 cup golden raisins
1 Tbsp honey
Juice of 1/2 lemon
3 cups cooked couscous
2 Tbsp toasted pine nuts
2 Tbsp chopped flat-leaf parsley

Directions

Dry the lamb and place it in a mixing bowl. Add the Greek seasoning, lemon zest, oregano and black pepper, and toss with your hands to coat all of the meat.

In a 5-quart Dutch oven, heat the olive oil over low heat. Arrange the meat in a single layer (in batches, if necessary), and brown the meat lightly on all sides. Stir in the garlic, and let it cook for 30 seconds; then add the wine, raisins and honey, plus the lemon juice. Reduce the heat to simmer, cover the pot, and cook for 1-1/4 hours, stirring occasionally. If the pan gets too dry and you think the meat will burn before it finishes cooking, add more wine or water, 1/4 cup at a time. You will end up with very dark lamb, caramelized on the outside, and a small amount of sauce. (Add water to thin the sauce at the end of the cooking, if you wish.) Serve over couscous, topped with toasted pine nuts and parsley.

Lentil salad with bell peppers, salmon, and maple-mustard dressing {gluten-free}

Serves 4-6 as a main course salad.

A complete meal in a bowl, great for potluck.

Ingredients

1 cup cooked brown lentils*
1 cup chopped bell peppers, a mix of colors
1 cup cooked salmon (broiled, grilled or steamed, optional; substitute 1 cup leftover chopped rotisserie chicken, or omit, for vegan)
2 Tbsp dried cranberries
2 Tbsp chopped flat-leaf parsley
2 Tbsp crumbled feta cheese (omit for vegan)

FOR THE DRESSING:
2 Tbsp maple syrup
2 Tbsp Dijon mustard
2 Tbsp white balsamic vinegar
1 garlic clove, minced (or use 1/2 tsp garlic paste from a tube)
Large pinch of black pepper
6 Tbsp extra virgin olive oil

Directions

Cook 3/4 cup of unsoaked lentils (to yield 1 cup cooked) in a pot of water, with enough water to cover by at least 2 inches. Bring the water to a boil, then reduce heat to simmer and cook, covered, for 25-30 minutes, until the lentils are soft but not falling apart. Drain, and cool. Refrigerate the cooked and cooled lentils until you're ready to use them.

Add the lentils to a large mixing bowl, along with bell peppers, salmon (or chicken), dried cranberries, parsley and feta.

In a small jar with a tight-fitting lid, combine all of the dressing ingredients. Shake the jar vigorously to emulsify (thicken) the dressing. Drizzle on as much vinaigrette dressing as you need to moisten the salad. Taste, and add salt and pepper, if needed. Serve at room temperature, or refrigerate and serve chilled.

For the story behind a recipe, and ingredient info, search the recipe name on www.theperfectpantry.com.

Light and easy sliced cucumber salad {vegan, gluten-free}

Serves 6; can be multiplied.

Spicy and tart, great with barbecue.

Ingredients

1 large English (seedless) cucumber
3/4 tsp kosher salt
1/4 cup rice vinegar
1/2 Tbsp sesame oil
1 packet artificial sweetener (I use Stevia), or 1 tsp honey or agave nectar
1/8 to 1/4 tsp mild red pepper flakes, to taste
1/8 tsp fresh black pepper

Directions

Using a mandoline set to 1/8-inch thickness, or a very sharp knife, slice the cucumber into thin rounds. Place the slices in a colander, and set the colander over a mixing bowl. Sprinkle the cucumbers with salt, making sure to toss them so the salt gets to each slice. Set aside on the counter for 30 minutes.

Combine remaining ingredients in another mixing bowl, and whisk together. Taste, and adjust seasoning if necessary. (Do not add salt!)

After 30 minutes, lift the colander out of the bowl, and shake over the sink to remove most of the moisture clinging to the cucumbers. Do not rinse, and do not pat dry.

Add the cucumbers to the bowl with the dressing, and stir gently to make sure the dressing reaches all of the slices. Wait 2 minutes, and stir again. Repeat for 10 minutes, then set aside at room temperature for 10 minutes. Stir again.

Serve right away, or cover the bowl and refrigerate for up to several hours and serve chilled. Can be made up to 2 days ahead.

Lobster, corn and basil quiche

Serves 6.

A luxurious quiche for a special meal.

Ingredients

1 refrigerated store-bought pie crust
1 Tbsp olive oil
1 leek, washed and trimmed, diced
3/4 cup roasted corn kernels, or fresh kernels from 1 ear of corn
8 oz cooked lobster meat or shelled, cooked langoustines, cut into 1/2-inch pieces
1/4 cup roughly chopped fresh basil leaves
5 large eggs
1/2 cup nonfat (skim) milk
2 Tbsp sour cream
8 oz grated mild cheese (I use Italian 6-cheese blend, store-bought; you can use a mix of any cheese you prefer)
1/2 tsp kosher salt
1/2 tsp fresh black pepper

Directions

Preheat oven to 350°F. Fit the pie crust into a 9-inch pie dish, and set aside.

In a small nonstick frying pan, heat the oil over medium-low heat. Add the leeks and corn, and cook for 2 minutes. Stir in the pieces of lobster, and cook for 1 minute. Turn the heat off, toss in the chopped basil, and remove the pan from heat.

In a large glass measuring cup (8-cup size) or mixing bowl, whisk together the eggs, milk and sour cream. Then, with a rubber spatula, stir in the cheese, salt and pepper. Add the cooked vegetables and lobster to the eggs, and stir to combine. Pour the mixture into the prepared pie crust.

Bake for 35-40 minutes, until the top is slightly browned and the quiche is firm to the touch. Remove the pan from the oven and set it on a wire rack to cool for at least 15 minutes, or until room temperature.

Slice and serve, or let the quiche cool completely, cover with plastic wrap, and refrigerate for up to 2 days.

Lorna's sour cream cake

Serves 8-10.

A reader's recipe makes the best cake.

Ingredients

2 cups all-purpose unbleached flour
1 tsp baking powder
1 tsp baking soda
1/4 lb (1 stick) butter, softened
1-1/3 cup granulated sugar, divided
2 large eggs
1 tsp vanilla extract
1 cup (8 oz) sour cream
1 Tbsp cinnamon
Baking spray

Directions

Preheat oven to 350°F. (Note: if using a ceramic pan, DO NOT PREHEAT the oven.) Spray the inside of a small (5-cup) Bundt pan or loaf pan with baking spray, and set aside. A tip Lorna shared: if you're using a Bundt pan, roll a small piece of parchment paper, an inch or so taller than the pan; place the pan on a sheet pan, and insert the parchment paper in the hole. If the cake rises above the top of the pan, it won't slide down in the center. (You can see that I did this, in the top photograph on the blog.)

In a mixing bowl, stir together the flour, baking powder and baking soda.

In the bowl of a Kitchenaid-type stand mixer, cream together the butter, 1 cup of sugar, and the eggs, until the eggs turn light yellow. Stir in the vanilla. Add to the egg mixture, alternating, the dry ingredients and sour cream.

Pour half of the batter into the prepared pan, and spread evenly.

In a small bowl, stir together the remaining 1/3 cup of sugar and the cinnamon. Sprinkle this over the batter in the pan, and top with the remaining batter.

Bake at 350F for 45 minutes (if using a ceramic pan, place the pan in a cold oven, set to 350F, and bake for 60 minutes), or until a tester comes out clean.

Set the pan on a wire rack to cool for 15 minutes, then invert the pan and remove the cake. Let it cool completely. Serve, or wrap and freeze.

Lydia's very famous jambalaya

Serves 6-8.

Spicy, oh-so-comforting, and justly famous.

Ingredients

3 Tbsp butter
1 lb hot smoked sausage , sliced into 1/4-inch rounds
2 onions, chopped (3/4-inch – fairly large)
1 large green bell pepper, chopped (same as onion)
3 stalks celery, chopped (same as onion)
1-1/2 lb boneless, skinless chicken breast, cut into 1-inch pieces
4-6 cloves garlic, minced, or a large dollop of crushed garlic in a jar
1 handful dried oregano (approx 1-1/2 Tbsp)
1/2 handful dried thyme leaf (approx 3/4 Tbsp)
4 large dried bay leaves
1 Tbsp black pepper
Hot sauce, to taste (from 4 drops to 4 ounces)
8 oz tomato sauce (1 small can)
1 lb chopped or diced canned tomatoes
2 cups chicken stock (homemade or low-sodium store-bought)
2 cups long grain white rice
1 lb peeled, deveined large shrimp, 26-30 size (optional)

Directions

Preheat oven to 350°F.

In a 6-quart or 8-quart stock pot, melt butter over medium heat. Add sausage, and cook, stirring occasionally, until quite brown and sticking to the bottom of the pot, approximately 10 minutes. Add onion, green pepper and celery, and cook, stirring, 5 minutes or until onion is translucent.

Turn heat to high, and add chicken. Stir frequently, 2-3 minutes, until chicken is "seized" (no longer pink on the outside). Reduce heat to medium-low, stir in garlic, oregano, thyme, bay leaves and black pepper, and stir 1-2 minutes. Add hot sauce, and cook for 1 minute. Add tomato sauce and tomatoes. Stir to combine, and cover.

Cook 8-10 minutes, stirring once. Uncover, add chicken stock, and bring to the boil. Stir in the rice.

Cover the pot, and place in the oven. Bake for 1 hour. (Add shrimp after the jambalaya has been baking for 50 minutes.)

Turn off oven, and let pot sit for at least 5 minutes before serving.

Mee goreng (spicy fried noodles)

Serves 4-5 as part of a family-style meal, 2-3 as a main dish.

My breakfast every morning in Malaysia.

Ingredients

2 cups fresh Chinese egg noodles
2 Tbsp vegetable oil
2 eggs
1 cup mung bean sprouts
1/2 cup shredded cabbage
1/4 lb shrimp, peeled and deveined
1/4 lb boneless chicken breast, cubed (or leftover cooked chicken)
1 tsp minced garlic
2 Tbsp chili sauce (Sriracha), or more to taste
1 tsp dark soy sauce
1 tsp sugar
1/4 tsp salt
3 Tbsp oyster sauce
3 Tbsp ketchup
2 Tbsp shao hsing wine, or more to taste
1/4 tsp white pepper
2 Tbsp scallions, sliced
2 Tbsp fried shallots (available packaged at Asian markets)

Directions

Bring a large pot of water to a boil. Cook the noodles for 30 seconds, drain, and rinse with cold water. Set aside. In a large preheated wok, add the vegetable oil. Crack the eggs into the wok, stir vigorously until the eggs are just set, then add the garlic, noodles, bean sprouts, cabbage, shrimp, chicken, and 3/4 cup water. Stir-fry continuously until noodles are cooked, 3-5 minutes (depending on the heat of your wok). Add chili sauce, dark soy, sugar, salt, oyster sauce and ketchup, and continue stirring. The noodles should begin to get a bit drier. Add shao hsing wine and white pepper, stir to combine, and remove from heat. Garnish with scallions and fried shallots.

Moroccan eggplant salad {vegan, gluten-free}

Serves 4.

You'll love the fresh herbs in this salad.

Ingredients

2 eggplants (unpeeled), ends trimmed, sliced into 1/2-inch thick rounds
Kosher salt
Olive oil for frying
6 whole scallions, minced
1 tomato, minced
2 huge garlic cloves, minced
1/2 cup minced fresh herbs -- a mix of parsley and cilantro
Juice of 1-1/2 lemons
1-2 Tbsp extra-virgin olive oil
Fresh ground black pepper, to taste

Directions

Place eggplant slices in a colander, and toss with a generous amount (a couple of teaspoons) of kosher salt. Set the colander over a bowl or plate, and let stand for 30 minutes, then rinse the eggplant and dry well.

In a frying pan filmed with olive oil, saute the eggplant over medium heat until cooked through but not crispy brown, approximately 8 minutes. Drain on paper towels.

Dice eggplant and place in a bowl with remaining ingredients. Mix thoroughly (with your hands -- the eggplant should break down), and set aside to marinate for several hours at room temperature.

Can be made up to 1 day ahead.

Oven-barbecued brisket

Serves 12, in theory, though everyone always eats more than they think possible.

A completely addictive recipe from Peggy.

Ingredients

9 lbs flat-cut beef brisket, in two pieces, most fat removed
1 tsp minced garlic (good quality from a jar is fine)
1 tsp celery seeds
3 Tbsp freshly ground black pepper
1 tsp ground ginger
4 large bay leaves, crumbled
12 oz tomato paste
1 cup dark soy sauce
1/2 cup Worcestershire sauce
1 cup tightly packed dark brown sugar
2 medium onion thinly sliced
1 bottle beer

Directions

Preheat oven to 350°F.

Trim brisket and rub all over with the garlic. Combine celery seeds, pepper, ginger and bay leaves, then rub into all sides of the brisket. Mix the tomato paste, soy, Worcestershire and sugar, and smear this all over the meat. Score the fat side of the brisket and place the onions on top, and place the meat in a heavy nonstick high-sided roasting pan. Cover tightly with aluminum foil. Cook for 4 hours. Open the foil to expose the onion-covered top, and cook for another hour.

Remove meat to a heated plate and keep warm. Place the roasting pan on the stovetop over medium-high heat, and degrease sauce with the bottle of beer until the sauce has reduced to a pleasant consistency. [Note: Though it's truly delicious right out of the oven, the flavor improves if cooked a day ahead; refrigerate in the sauce, and slice cold.] Serve at room temperature, or reheat.

Penne with red pepper pesto {vegan}

Serves 6.

Not all pesto is green!

Ingredients

1 lb penne (or pasta of your choice)
1/2 cup pine nuts
12 oz roasted red peppers (I use good quality store-bought)
1/2 cup firmly packed fresh parsley leaves (reserve a few leaves for garnish)
3 Tbsp olive oil
1 Tbsp balsamic vinegar
1 pinch of mild red pepper flakes (optional, to taste)
2 cloves garlic, peeled
1/4 tsp kosher salt
1/8 tsp ground black pepper

Directions

Bring a large pot of water to boil, and cook pasta according to package directions.

While the pasta is cooking, toast the pine nuts in a dry nonstick frying pan over medium heat for 2-3 minutes, shaking or stirring frequently, until the nuts are just lightly browned. Add the nuts to the food processor, along with all remaining ingredients. Blend until smooth. (Can be made ahead.)

Drain the pasta, but do not rinse. Add to a large bowl with as much of the pesto as you like to coat the pasta, and stir to combine. Garnish with reserved parsley leaves. Serve hot or at room temperature.

Picadillo black bean and rice salad with chicken and olives {gluten-free, can be vegetarian}

Serves 4; can be multiplied.

A little bit tangy, a little bit sweet.

Ingredients

FOR THE SALAD:
1 boneless, skinless chicken breast
2 Tbsp extra virgin olive oil
2 cups cooked brown rice at room temperature (if using leftover rice, microwave for 1 minute to bring it to room temperature)
1 cup cooked or canned black beans
1 cup small green olives stuffed with pimiento
1/4 cup raisins or prunes
1 tsp capers

FOR THE VINAIGRETTE:
2 Tbsp extra virgin olive oil
1 clove garlic, chopped
1/4 cup white wine vinegar
1/4 cup sherry vinegar
1 tsp agave nectar
Pinch of salt

Directions

In a small nonstick frying pan, heat the oil over medium heat. Sauté the chicken until just done, but not overly browned. Remove chicken from the pan, and when cool enough, chop into bite-size pieces. Add to a large mixing bowl. Set the pan with the oil aside. Combine remaining salad ingredients in the mixing bowl.

Return the frying pan to the stove, and set the heat to low. Pour in the vinaigrette ingredients. Raise heat to medium, and whisk gently to combine all of the ingredients. "Cook" the dressing for 2-3 minutes, then pour it over the salad. Toss gently to coat all of the salad with the dressing. Serve at room temperature, or refrigerate, covered, for up to a few hours. When it's time to serve, microwave the salad for a minute to soften the rice.

Pie-ella

Serves 6.

If you like risotto, you'll love this easy "paella".

Ingredients

1 large pinch saffron threads
2 Tbsp olive oil
3 hot smoked sausages (I use Beef Hot Links), cut on a diagonal into large chunks; substitute your favorite spicy sausage)
3/4 lb boneless, skinless chicken breast, cut into large chunks
1 medium red onion, cut in quarters
1/2 green bell pepper, cut into large chunks
1/2 red bell pepper, cut into large chunks
1 cup dry white wine
2 cups chicken stock (I use Swanson 99%; if you use homemade, you'll need to add salt)
1 cup carnaroli or arborio rice
18 pitted black jumbo olives (use canned olives, because you don't want a strong flavor)
18 large (21-25 size) shrimp, peeled and deveined
Lots of black pepper to taste

Directions

Soak the saffron in 1 cup hot water for 15 minutes. Then, put on an apron -- the first steps in this cooking are messy.

In a 4- or 6-quart stockpot, heat the olive oil. Add sausage chunks, and brown all over. Using long tongs, remove sausage from pan into a small bowl. Add chicken, brown all over and remove from pan into another small bowl. The pan will be black and gunky, but don't worry -- this will all dissolve into the finished dish.

Add onion, green and red peppers, and sauté quickly until the onion is just translucent, about 2 minutes. Return the sausage to the pan, add the saffron water with saffron, wine and 1-1/2 cups of the stock.

When the liquid boils, turn down to low. Add the rice, stir once, and cook for 5 minutes. Add the chicken back into the pan, along with the olives.
Now, don't stir for a while. Go away, drink some wine, make a salad.

Continue to simmer, uncovered, until the rice is nearly cooked, about 10 minutes or more. There should still be liquid in the rice, but not much. Run a spatula along the bottom of the pan to loosen any stuck bits of rice. Add the shrimp, making sure to stuff them down into the rice. Season with lots of black pepper.

From this point, you may have to use your spatula along the bottom of the pan every now and then to keep the rice from sticking, and if it is cooking too fast, add the remaining 1/2 cup chicken stock. Continue cooking until the shrimp are done, approximately 5 minutes or so.

Serve hot.

Polenta with wild mushroom ragout {vegetarian}

Serves 6-8.

An impressive meatless dish for entertaining.

Ingredients

1 large onion, chopped fine
4 cloves garlic, minced
1 tsp dried rosemary, crumbled, or 2 tsp minced fresh rosemary, or 2 tsp fresh thyme leaves
4 Tbsp olive oil
1 lb cremini or white mushrooms sliced thin
1 lb fresh shiitake mushrooms, stems discarded, quartered
1 Tbsp tomato paste
1 cup dry red wine
1 Tbsp cornstarch
1-1/3 cups mushroom broth (or beef broth)
2 tsp Worcestershire sauce
6 cups water
2 cups yellow cornmeal
2 Tbsp unsalted butter, cut into pieces
1 cup grated Parmigiano-Reggiano cheese
1/3 cup minced fresh flat-leaf parsley
1/4 lb mozzarella cheese, shredded

Directions

Preheat oven to 400°F. Spray a 3-quart casserole dish or clay cazuela with cooking spray (like PAM) and set aside. Spray a sheet pan with cooking spray and set that aside, too.

Make the mushroom ragout: In a large deep skillet, heat 3 Tbsp olive oil over medium heat. Cook onion, garlic and rosemary, stirring occasionally until the onion is softened. Add mushrooms and salt to taste, and cook over moderately high heat, stirring, for 10 minutes or until the liquid the mushrooms gives off is evaporated. Stir in tomato paste and the wine, and boil until most of the liquid is evaporated. In a small bowl stir the cornstarch into the broth, add the mixture and the Worcestershire sauce to the mushroom mixture (this is now the ragout), and bring it to a boil, stirring. Reduce heat to simmer and cook 2 minutes. Season with salt and pepper to taste. Turn off the heat and set aside.

Make the polenta: In a large, heavy saucepan, bring the water with 1 Tbsp olive oil to a boil and add 1 cup of the cornmeal, a little at a time, whisking constantly. Reduce heat to low, add the remaining 1 cup cornmeal in a slow stream, stirring constantly, and bring mixture to a boil. Remove pan from the heat and with a wooden spoon stir in the butter, 2/3 cup of the parmesan, the parsley, and salt and pepper to taste.

Spread 1/3 of the polenta on the sheet pan to 1/4 inch thick, and chill for 20 minutes, or until it is firm. While it is chilling, working quickly, spread half the remaining polenta in the prepared casserole dish or cazuela, top it with half the mushroom ragout, and top the ragout with the mozzarella. Spread the remaining polenta quickly over the mozzarella and top with the remaining ragout.

Invert the polenta sheet onto a work surface and with one or more star-shaped (or any other shape) cookie cutters, cut out as many stars as possible (use different sizes for a nice effect). Arrange the stars decoratively on the ragout and sprinkle with the remaining parmesan. The dish may be prepared up to this point and refrigerated, covered, for up to 2 days.

Bake uncovered in the upper third of the oven for 30-40 minutes, or until the polenta stars are golden.

Serve hot.

Pressure cooker (or stovetop) pozole verde beef stew {gluten-free}

Serves 4.

Make this Mexican-inspired stew hot or mild.

Ingredients

1 lb stew beef (chuck roast), cut into 1-inch cubes
1/2 tsp ground cumin
1/2 tsp garlic powder
1/2 tsp kosher salt
1/2 tsp fresh black pepper
1/8-1/4 tsp cayenne pepper, to taste (use less if you don't like a lot of heat)
1 small onion, diced
1 clove garlic, minced
16 oz green salsa, store-bought (I like Herdez brand) or homemade (mild to hot: your choice)
15-oz can white or yellow hominy (also called pozole), drained and rinsed
2 tsp cornstarch, mixed with 4 tsp water
Juice of 1 lime
Fresh cilantro, for garnish
Fresh avocado, for garnish (optional)

Directions

In a mixing bowl, combine the beef, cumin, garlic powder, salt, black pepper and cayenne. Mix well to distribute the spices to all pieces of the beef.

Place the beef in your pressure cooker (I use a 6-quart electric pressure cooker or Instant Pot), and add the onion, garlic, salsa and hominy. Stir everything together.

[Note: for stovetop cooking, do exactly the same thing. Add the beef and other ingredients to a Dutch oven, along with 1 cup of water or beef stock, and cook on low-medium heat for 1-1/4 hours. Check periodically, and add more stock or water if the sauce is reducing too quickly before the beef is cooked through. If the beef hasn't cooked through, cook for 15 minutes or as long as necessary.]

Lock the top of the pressure cooker and cook on HIGH PRESSURE for 22 minutes. Then, NATURAL PRESSURE RELEASE for 10 minutes, and Quick Release remaining pressure. Turn the pressure cooker off when the pressure valve drops.

Carefully open the lid. Set the pressure cooker to Sauté, and when the stew comes to a boil, stir in the cornstarch mixture. The stew will thicken slightly. Turn off the cooker.

Ladle the pozole into individual serving bowls. Garnish with a squirt of lime and some fresh cilantro. (If you wish, you could also add sliced radishes and avocado for garnish.)

Serve hot.

Quick and easy black beans and rice {vegan, gluten-free}

Serves 4-6.

I love black beans and rice for a main course.

Ingredients

2 tsp canola oil
1 small onion, peeled and chopped
1 clove garlic, peeled and chopped
1 tsp ground cumin
1 tsp ground chili powder (I like Penzeys Chili 3000)
2 oz canned roasted green chile peppers (half a small can)
2 cups *cooked* white rice
1/4 cup red sofrito (available in supermarkets, in the Latino foods section)
1 15-oz can black beans, rinsed and drained
1/4 tsp kosher salt
1/4 tsp black pepper

Directions

In a large nonstick frying pan, heat the oil over medium-low heat. Add the onion, and cook 2-3 minutes, until soft and translucent. Stir in the garlic, cumin, chili powder and green chile peppers, and cook for 2 minutes.

If the rice is cold, break it up with your hands as you add it to the pot. Stir well to combine the rice and onion mixture; cook, stirring, for 2-3 minutes until the rice is warmed through. Add in the sofrito and black beans, and stir gently, until the sofrito is incorporated and the beans evenly distributed throughout the rice.

Season with the salt and pepper. Taste, and add more if needed.

Serve warm, or cool completely and refrigerate. You can make this up to 2 days in advance; add a few drops of water and reheat in the microwave.

Quick and easy chilled miso noodles with broccoli, bell pepper and peanuts {vegan}

Serves 4; can be multiplied.

My granddaughters love these noodles.

Ingredients

8 oz dry linguine or spaghetti
2 Tbsp miso paste
1 Tbsp reduced-sodium soy sauce
1 Tbsp mirin
2 tsp agave nectar
1 tsp sesame oil
Juice of 1/2 lime
1/8 tsp grated fresh ginger root
2 cups chopped broccoli florets
1 small red bell pepper, diced
2 Tbsp chopped peanuts (or cashews)

Directions

In a large pot, bring 6 quarts of water to boil. Add the pasta, and when the water returns to the boil, reduce the heat to low and cook for 6 minutes, or until the noodles taste cooked through but still have some texture. Drain, run under cool water to stop the cooking, and drain again.

While the noodles are cooking, whisk together in a large mixing bowl the miso, soy sauce, mirin, agave nectar, sesame oil, lime juice and ginger.

Add the cooked noodles to the miso sauce, and stir to combine while the noodles are still a bit warm.

Then, toss in the broccoli, bell pepper and chopped peanuts. Mix again.

Serve at room temperature, or refrigerate and serve chilled.

Quinoa salad with roasted sweet potato, apples, dried cranberries and pine nuts {vegan, gluten-free}

Serves 6.

All the colors and flavors of autumn.

Ingredients

1 cup quinoa
1 large sweet potato, peeled and diced
3 Tbsp cider vinegar
4 Tbsp extra virgin olive oil, divided
1/4 tsp kosher salt
1/4 tsp fresh black pepper
1 small red onion, thinly sliced
1 Granny Smith apple, diced (do not peel)
1 firm red apple, diced (do not peel)
3/4 cup dried cranberries
1/2 cup pine nuts

Directions

Preheat oven to 425°F.

Rinse and drain the quinoa, and place it in a rice cooker. Fill the cooker to the 1 cup mark, and set to cook. (Or, cook on the stovetop, according to package directions.) When the quinoa is cooked, turn off the cooker and allow the quinoa to steam, with the top closed, for 15 minutes. (Or, on stovetop, remove pot from the heat and set aside, covered, for 15 minutes.) Scrape the quinoa into a large mixing bowl, and let cool while you prepare the remaining ingredients.

Place the diced sweet potato on a rimmed baking sheet. Sprinkle with salt and pepper, and toss with 1 tablespoon of olive oil. Roast for 15-20 minutes, until just tender and starting to brown slightly. Remove from the oven, and set aside.

WHILE THE SWEET POTATO IS COOKING, stir together the red onion with 1 teaspoon of olive oil in a small frying pan. Cook over lowest heat for 8-10 minutes, until the onion is very soft and beginning to brown slightly. Set aside.

In a large mixing bowl, whisk together the vinegar, 3 tablespoons of olive oil, salt and pepper, until the dressing emulsifies (thickens). Toss in the quinoa, sweet potato, onion, diced apple and cranberries.

In the same frying pan in which you cooked the onion, toast the pine nuts for 3-4 minutes over medium heat, until the nuts begin to brown. Add those to the mixing bowl, and gently toss to bring all of the ingredients together.

Serve warm or at room temperature.

Red curry beef with mushrooms, red bell pepper and cilantro

Serves 4.

When I crave Thai flavors, I make curry beef.

Ingredients

1 lb ground beef (93% lean)
1/2 tsp fresh lime juice
2 tsp brown sugar
2 Tbsp fish sauce (I use Three Crabs brand)
1 small bunch of scallions (6-8), thinly sliced
1 small red bell pepper, diced
4 large white mushrooms, sliced
A scant 1/4 cup Thai red curry paste (I use Mae Ploy brand)
6 oz coconut milk
2 tsp cilantro, roughly chopped

Directions

In a wok or deep frying pan set over medium heat, brown the beef, breaking it up with a spatula as it cooks. (Don't add any fat to the pan; the meat will render enough fat to cook.)

In a small bowl, mix together the lime juice, brown sugar and fish sauce, and set aside.

When the beef is browned, raise the heat to medium-high, and add the scallions, red bell pepper and mushrooms to the pan. Stir-fry for 2 minutes, until the pepper is just warmed through. Add the curry paste to the wok, and stir for 1 minute. Then, pour in the coconut milk, and stir to combine. Let the dish simmer for 1 minute, and pour in the fish sauce mixture. Stir for 1 minute.

Serve over rice or lettuce leaves. Garnish with cilantro, and serve hot or at room temperature.

Risotto with shrimp and asparagus

Serves 4 as a main course.

A classic risotto, in gorgeous Spring colors.

Ingredients

1 tsp olive oil
1/2 lb large shrimp, peeled and deveined
6 stalks asparagus, trimmed, cut into 1-inch pieces3 cups chicken broth (homemade stock or low-sodium store-bought)
1/2 cup water
1/4 tsp saffron threads
2-3 Tbsp olive oil
1/3 cup finely minced onion
1 cups carnaroli or arborio rice
1/2 cup dry white wine
1 Tbsp unsalted butter
1/4 cup Parmigiano-Reggiano cheese, grated
Fresh ground black pepper, to taste

Directions

In a small nonstick frying pan, heat 1 tsp olive oil. Sauté the shrimp and asparagus for 2-3 minutes, until the shrimp just curls and turns pink. Remove from the pan to a bowl, and set aside while you make the rice.

Bring broth to a boil on the stovetop or in a microwave, and set aside. Place 1/2 cup water and the saffron threads into a small glass measuring cup; heat in the microwave for 1 minute, then set aside. Heat remaining oil in a large, deep skillet or 4-quart straight-sided pan. Add the onion, and sauté until soft but not brown, 2-3 minutes. Stir in the rice, making sure to coat each grain, and stir until the rice just begins to turn light brown.

Remove the pan from the heat, and stir in the wine. It will bubble up, so be careful. Return the pan to the heat. When the liquid is absorbed, begin adding broth, 1 ladleful at a time, letting each bit of liquid be absorbed. After 1 cup is added, stir the saffron water into the rice. Continue adding broth, reserving a few tablespoons at the end. Remove from heat. Add butter and cheese, and stir vigorously for 2 minutes. Add in any remaining broth, and stir to desired creaminess. Stir in the shrimp and asparagus. Season to taste with black pepper, and serve immediately.

Roasted asparagus with Sriracha drizzle {vegetarian}

Serves 4.

I love this creamy, spicy sauce on asparagus.

Ingredients

1 lb thin asparagus spears, ends trimmed
1 tsp olive oil
A pinch each of kosher salt and fresh black pepper
2 Tbsp mayonnaise
1/4 tsp granulated sugar
1/4 to 1/2 tsp Sriracha sauce, to taste (start with 1/4 tsp)
1 tsp reduced sodium soy sauce
1/4 tsp rice vinegar

Directions

Preheat the oven to 450°F. Line a rimmed baking sheet with aluminum foil.

Spread the asparagus in a single layer on the baking sheet. Add the olive oil, and a pinch each of salt and pepper. Toss gently with your hands to distribute the seasonings, and return the asparagus to a single layer.

Roast for 10 minutes.

While the asparagus is in the oven, make the drizzle by combining the remaining ingredients in a small measuring cup with a pouring spout. Or, if you have a squeeze bottle, make a paper funnel out of wax paper or parchment, and transfer the drizzle to the squeeze bottle.

When the asparagus is done, arrange it on a serving plate, and squirt or pour the drizzle here and there.

Serve warm or at room temperature.

Salsa turkey meatball lettuce wraps

Makes 20-22 meatballs; serves 8-10 in lettuce wraps.

My husband Ted created these meatballs.

Ingredients

1 lb ground turkey (I use 93% fat-free)
1/2 cup plain dried bread crumbs
1/2 cup + 1 Tbsp bottled salsa verde, drained in a fine-mesh sieve (I love Herdez salsa verde)
1 Tbsp cumin
1 Tbsp chili powder
1/4 tsp cayenne pepper (optional)
1/4 tsp kosher salt
1/4 tsp fresh black pepper
1 large egg
1 Tbsp oil (any type: olive, vegetable, peanut, etc.)
1-2 heads romaine lettuce
1-1/2 cups cooked (or canned and drained) black beans
2-3 avocados, cubed
1-1/2 cups shredded cheese (I use low-fat 4-cheese Mexican blend)
Your favorite salsa, for garnish
Fresh cilantro leaves, to taste

Directions

In a large mixing bowl, combine turkey, bread crumbs, drained salsa, cumin, chili powder, salt and pepper, and the egg and oil. Mix well with your hands, just until all ingredients are combined (do not overmix). Set aside. [If you want to test for seasoning, brown a spoon-sized piece in a nonstick frying pan, and taste the cooked piece. Do not taste raw turkey. Adjust seasoning if needed.]

Preheat oven to 425°F. Line a rimmed baking sheet with a Silpat (silicone baking sheet) or parchment paper.

Using an ice cream scoop with a release (a disher), or a spoon, form the turkey mixture into 20-22 small meatballs, and place on the prepared baking sheet.

Bake for 18 minutes, and remove from the oven. Let cool to room temperature, or cool completely, pack into airtight containers, and refrigerate or freeze.

Begin the assembly of the lettuce wraps (you could use tortillas instead): Set out the lettuce leaves. Drizzle some black beans in each leaf. Top with 2-3 turkey meatballs. Add a few pieces of avocado, some cheese, a few drops of salsa, and cilantro leaves.

Serve at room temperature.

Salt cod balls (bolinhos de bacalhau) with chipotle dipping sauce

Adapted from *Brazil: A Cook's Tour*. Makes approximately 24 bolinhos, serving 6 people.

A very popular bar snack we enjoyed in Brazil.

Ingredients

1 lb salt cod
2 medium baking (Idaho) potatoes, peeled and cut into 4-6 chunks each
1 Tbsp minced onion
2 Tbsp minced flat-leaf parsley leaves
1 clove garlic, minced
Lots of fresh black pepper
2 large eggs, separated
1 Tbsp all-purpose flour
1 Tbsp kosher salt
1 cup plain dry bread crumbs
Vegetable or canola oil, for frying
1 cup mayonnaise
1/2 chipotle pepper in adobo sauce, minced, or 2-3 Tbsp of the adobo sauce

Directions

*Soak the salt cod in a bowl of cold water in the refrigerator for 48 hours, changing the water 5 or 6 times.

Drain the salt cod. Place in a small pot of cold water with 1 Tbsp white cider vinegar or rice vinegar. Bring to a low boil and cook for 15 minutes. Drain, and set aside until cool enough to handle. Then, pick the skin and bones from the fish, and add the fish to a large mixing bowl.

Bring a small pot of water to boil; add the potatoes and cook until tender, 15-20 minutes. Drain and cool slightly, then add to the mixing bowl along with onion, parsley, garlic, egg yolks, pepper, and flour. Mash all together with a masher or wooden spoon, and mix to combine.

In another large bowl, beat the egg whites with a whisk until stiff peaks are formed. Gently fold the egg whites into the cod mixture; try not to deflate the egg whites. Season with salt.

Place the bread crumbs in a bowl. Form the salt cod mixture into balls the size of a walnut, and gently coat with the bread crumbs. Place on a platter, and cover with plastic wrap. Refrigerate for 1 hour or more, until ready to cook. Don't skip this step; the bolinhos are delicate and need time to set, or they'll fall apart in the frying.

Make the dipping sauce by mixing together mayonnaise and adobo sauce (or minced chipotles) until you like the taste, mild or spicy. Place in a serving bowl, cover and refrigerate, for at least 1 hour or more (can be made a day or two ahead of time).

When you're ready to cook, fill a very deep, heavy saucepan with 1-1/2 inches of oil. (At the same time, remove the bolinhos from the refrigerator.)

Set the heat under the pan to high, and heat the oil until it reaches 350F or until it shimmers. One good way to test the oil is to stand a bamboo chopstick vertically with the eating tip down in the oil; if small bubbles appear at the base, the oil is hot enough.

Carefully fry the balls a few at a time, turning them a bit to make sure they brown all over, for 4-5 minutes. Remove with a slotted spoon or spider, onto a plate covered with paper towels.

If desired, sprinkle with coarse sea salt. Serve at room temperature.

Shakshuka: eggs in fiery tomato sauce {vegetarian, gluten-free}

Serves 2-3; recipe makes enough sauce for 4-6.

We love this with crusty bread for mopping up.

Ingredients

1/4 cup extra virgin olive oil
1 small onion, diced
2 cloves garlic, minced
1 large red bell pepper, diced
1 tsp ground cumin
1 tsp sweet paprika
1/2 tsp mild red pepper flakes, or more to taste
4-oz can roasted green chiles, or 1 small jalapeño pepper, seeds and ribs removed, minced
2 Tbsp tomato paste
28 oz canned chopped tomatoes, with their juices
1/2 tsp kosher salt
Fresh black pepper, to taste
3 large eggs
2-4 Tbsp roughly chopped fresh parsley

Directions

Heat the oil in a large nonstick frying pan over low-medium heat. When the oil is hot, add the onion, and sauté for 2-3 minutes, until soft. Add the garlic and red bell pepper, and continue to cook, stirring frequently, for 4-5 minutes, until the onion is translucent.

Stir in the cumin, paprika, and red pepper flakes. Mix well, and let the spices cook for 30 seconds. Then, pour in the green chiles (or jalapeño), and cook that for 30 seconds. Next, add the tomato paste, and stir that into the mixture.

Finally, add the chopped tomatoes. Reduce heat to simmer, and cook, stirring often, for 15 minutes, or until the sauce comes together and reduces. When most of the liquid has evaporated, remove the pan from the heat. At this point, you could let all of the sauce cool completely, and refrigerate or freeze it in airtight containers. {

Transfer half of the sauce into a smaller nonstick frying pan (I used a 9-inch size in the photos here). If the sauce has cooled, warm it over lowest heat until it is just below the simmer.

While the sauce is warming, crack each egg into its own small bowl. If there are any pieces of shell, now is the time to remove them.

Make 3 small indentations in the sauce, and gently slide an egg into each one. Cover the pan, and cook until the eggs are as runny, or firm, as you like them (I cook mine for 10 minutes, covered, which makes a somewhat runny egg).

Garnish with chopped parsley, and serve right away.

Shish taouk (garlic chicken on skewers) {gluten-free}

Serves 6-8.

The recipe that launched my food writing career.

Ingredients

6 boneless, skinless chicken breasts
2-4 cloves garlic, sliced, PLUS 4 cloves mashed (or from a jar)
1 tsp kosher salt
1/2 tsp pepper
1/2 tsp ground allspice
1/4 cup freshly squeezed lemon juice
1/4 cup olive oil

Directions

Wash chicken and pat dry with paper towels. Cut into 1-inch pieces. Add remaining ingredients, and mix well (with your hands). Marinate, covered or in a zip-loc bag, in the refrigerator for 4-5 hours, or overnight.

Heat grill to high. Place chicken on skewers, or on a barbecue grid, and cook over direct heat for 10-15 minutes, turning frequently.

Serve with rice or in pitas, with chopped iceberg lettuce, tomato and cucumber.

Shrimp, lemon, herb and feta macaroni and cheese

Serves 6-8.

The best mac and cheese ever. I promise.

Ingredients

13.25 oz rotini (I use Dreamfields low-carb)
1 lb frozen large shrimp, 31-40 size
2/3 lb feta, crumbled, divided (If you use Greek feta, be sure to taste your sauce before adding salt.)
3/4 cup panko
Zest of 2 large lemons, divided
4 Tbsp chopped flat-leaf parsley, divided
4 Tbsp butter
1/2 cup all-purpose unbleached flour
4 cups milk (whole or 2%)
1/2 lb gruyere or fontiago or Danish fontina, grated (or chopped in a food processor)
2 Tbsp chopped fresh dill weed
1/2 to 1 tsp kosher salt
1/2 to 1 tsp fresh black pepper

Directions

Bring a large stockpot of water to the boil, and add the pasta. Cook for 8 minutes; the pasta should be a bit underdone. Drain, rinse under cold water, and drain again. Add the pasta to a large mixing bowl and set aside.

Preheat oven to 400°F.

Remove shrimp from the freezer, and set in a bowl of cold water.

In a small bowl, combine 1/3 cup of the feta, half of the lemon zest, all of the panko and 2 Tbsp parsley. Mix well and set aside.

Peel and devein the shrimp as soon as they are defrosted enough to handle (but not fully defrosted) and add to the pasta.

Make the sauce: In a small sauce pan over medium heat, melt the butter. Add in the flour and stir until the flour is absorbed by the butter to form a paste. Cook, stirring, for 1 minute. Add the milk, and, with a wire whisk, stir vigorously to remove any lumps.

Continue to cook over medium heat, stirring frequently with the whisk, for 5 minutes or until the sauce thickens enough to coat the back of a wooden spoon.

Remove pot from heat, and whisk into the sauce the gruyere and the remaining feta. Whisk until the sauce is smooth; the gruyere will melt completely, and the feta will be well incorporated. Add the remaining lemon zest, the remaining parsley, dill weed, and salt and pepper to taste. Pour the sauce on top of the pasta, and stir to combine.

Pour the mixture into a casserole dish (approximately 9x13 inches). Sprinkle the panko mixture on top.

Place in the middle of the oven and bake, uncovered, for 25 minutes, until the top is browned and the cheese is bubbling a bit along the edges.

Remove from the oven, let sit for 5 minutes, and serve hot.

Slow cooker black bean and sweet potato stew {vegan, gluten-free}

Serves 4-6.

A great vegan dish for entertaining.

Ingredients

2 Tbsp olive oil
2 cups finely chopped onions
2 Tbsp minced fresh ginger root
2 tsp chili powder
1-1/2 tsp ground cumin
1-1/2 pounds red-skinned sweet potatoes (yams; about 2 medium), peeled, cut into 1/2-inch pieces
1-1/4 cups orange juice
2 Tbsp minced garlic
2 15- to 16-ounce cans black beans, rinsed, drained
1-2 chipotle chiles in adobo, chopped (to taste)
1 red bell pepper, chopped
Kosher salt and fresh black pepper, to taste
Toppings (optional): sour cream, diced avocado, orange or lime wedge

Directions

In a 5- or 6-quart slow cooker, add the olive oil, onions and ginger root. Turn the cooker to HIGH while you prepare the sweet potatoes.

Add the chili powder, cumin, sweet potato pieces, orange juice and garlic. Turn the cooker to LOW, cover, and cook for 3 hours.

After the potatoes have cooked and are nearly tender, stir in the black beans, chipotle chile peppers, bell pepper, and 1/2 teaspoon each of kosher salt and black pepper.

Cook on LOW for 1 hour, or until the sweet potatoes are cooked through. Taste, and adjust seasoning with more salt and pepper, if needed.

Serve hot. Can be made several days ahead.

Slow cooker Caribbean pepper pot {gluten-free}

Adapted from *Slow Cooker Comfort Food*, this recipe serves 6-8.

Use callaloo, if you can find it in the market.

Ingredients

1 Tbsp olive oil
2 large onions, cut in half and thinly sliced
4 cloves garlic, minced
2 Tbsp minced fresh ginger root
1 tsp kosher salt
1 tsp fresh black pepper
1 tsp allspice
1/2 tsp dried thyme leaves
2 bay leaves
1/2 cup Arborio rice
1 14-oz can diced tomatoes, with their juice
2 cups chicken stock (homemade or low-sodium store-bought)
4 cups cubed butternut squash (cut into 1-inch pieces)
1 lb boneless, skinless chicken thighs, cut into 1-inch cubes
4 cups chopped kale or callaloo
1 lb uncooked medium or large shrimp, peeled and deveined, cut in half if large
2-3 jalapeño peppers*
1 cup coconut milk

Directions

NOTE: I used my *6-quart Ninja slow cooker*, and prepared everything right in the cooker. If you have a Ninja or other cooker in which you can sauté, make the entire dish in the slow cooker instead of using a skillet for the first steps.

In a nonstick skillet, heat the oil over medium heat. Add the onions and cook, stirring frequently, for 3 minutes until just softened. Stir in the garlic, ginger, salt, pepper, allspice, thyme and bay leaves, and cook for 1 minute. Then add the rice, and toss until everything is combined.

Pour in the tomatoes, with their juice, plus the chicken stock, and bring the mixture to a boil.

For the story behind a recipe, and ingredient info, search the recipe name on www.theperfectpantry.com.

Transfer the mixture to a 5- or 6-quart slow cooker. Stir in the squash and chicken. Cover and cook on LOW for 5 hours. Lift the lid and stir once or twice during that time.

[*While the stew is cooking, prepare the hot peppers. The original recipe called for 1-2 habañero peppers, which would make this entirely fiery. Instead, I used 3 jalapeños. From 2 of the peppers, I removed the ribs and seeds. I left the ribs and seeds in the third pepper. This made a nicely spicy stew. If you don't love heat, try just one jalapeño with the ribs and seeds removed. Don't omit the pepper entirely, or you won't have a pepper pot!]

After 5 hours, open the cooker and stir in the kale, a bit at a time until it has all settled into the stew. Add the shrimp, jalapeño pepper, and coconut milk. Stir everything together; it will look strangely disconnected at this point, but don't worry.

Turn the cooker to HIGH. Cover and cook for 20 minutes, until the kale is wilted and the shrimp is pink. Stir well to incorporate everything. Remove and discard the bay leaves.

Serve hot, over rice

Slow cooker honey Sriracha beef stew

Serves 6-8.

My husband Ted loves this hearty stew.

Ingredients

1 cup dried mushrooms
2 lb stew beef (chuck, bottom round, etc.), cut into large chunks
2 cups all-purpose unbleached flour
2 Tbsp oil (olive, rice bran, vegetable, etc.)
3 cloves garlic, peeled and sliced
1-inch chunk of peeled ginger root
1 medium red onion, diced
4 medium carrots, peeled and sliced into 1/2-inch pieces
1/4 cup reduced-sodium soy sauce
1/4 cup oyster-flavored sauce
2 tsp rice vinegar
14-oz bag frozen pearl onions, defrosted
3 Tbsp honey
1/2 tsp Sriracha, or more to taste
Kosher salt and fresh black pepper, to taste

Directions

Place the dried mushrooms in a 2-cup glass measuring cup, and fill the cup with water. Microwave for 3 minutes. Remove, and set aside.

Dry the chunks of beef with paper towels. Add the flour to a large mixing bowl. Heat the oil in a nonstick frying pan (or in **a** slow cooker with a stovetop insert, or a Ninja cooker**).** Dredge the beef in the flour, shake off the excess, and brown the beef in the oil, in as many batches as necessary so the pan is not overcrowded. When all of the beef is browned, add it to the insert of a 5- or 6-quart slow cooker.

Stir in the garlic, ginger, onion, carrots, soy sauce, oyster sauce and rice vinegar. Drain the mushroom soaking liquid through a fine-mesh strainer, and add the liquid only to the slow cooker. (Save the reconstituted mushrooms for another use; you can freeze them, or chop and add to soup.)

Cover and cook on LOW for 4 hours.

Then, stir in the onions, honey and Sriracha. Cook on LOW for 1-1/2 hours.
Taste, and add salt and pepper as needed.

Using a slotted spoon, remove the beef and vegetables from the slow cooker into a large bowl. Pour the remaining sauce into a small saucepan. Reduce the sauce on the stovetop, over medium-high heat, for 10 minutes or until reduced by half. The sauce should be thicker, with a bit of sheen from the honey.

Pour the reduced sauce over the meat and vegetables, and stir to combine. Serve hot, with rice or noodles. Or, let cool completely and refrigerate or freeze.

Slow cooker sausage and four cheese lasagna

Serves 8-10. Can be frozen.

My new favorite way to cook lasagna.

Ingredients

FOR THE SAUCE:
1 lb lean ground beef or turkey
12 oz pre-cooked sausage (I like Aidells Italian-style chicken sausage with mozzarella cheese, garlic and basil), diced
1 medium onion, diced
2 cloves garlic, minced
1 28-oz box chopped tomatoes (I use Pomi brand)
1 14-oz can diced tomatoes
2 Tbsp tomato paste
2 Tbsp Dijon mustard
2 Tbsp chopped basil or herb paste from a tube
Kosher salt and fresh black pepper, to taste

FOR THE LASAGNA:
14 ruffle-edge dry lasagna noodles (do not pre-cook)
8 oz shredded low-fat mozzarella
2 cups nonfat cottage cheese
1-1/2 cups part-skim ricotta cheese
1-1/2 cups shredded or grated Parmigiano-Reggiano cheese, divided
1 large egg
2 Tbsp chopped basil or herb paste from a tube
Kosher salt and fresh black pepper, to taste

Directions

First, make the sauce (this can be done far in advance and refrigerated or frozen): In a Dutch oven or deep stock pot, brown the beef or turkey over low heat (do not add any oil to the pot). Stir frequently to break up the pieces of meat and keep it from sticking. When the meat is mostly brown, add the sausage and onion, and cook 4-5 minutes, until the sausage just begins to brown, and the onion is translucent. Stir in the garlic, and cook for 2 minutes.

Then, add the remaining sauce ingredients. Mix well, reduce the heat to simmer, and cook partially covered for 30-40 minutes, stirring occasionally, until the sauce has reduced and thickened a bit.

Set aside to cool for a few minutes, or make the sauce ahead and refrigerate or

To make the lasagna, spread 1 cup of sauce in the bottom of a 6-quart slow cooker. Top the sauce with a layer of dry noodles. Break the noodles as needed to cover the slow cooker insert.

Cover with another layer of sauce, approximately 1-1/2 cups.

In a mixing bowl, combine all of the cheeses (reserve 1/2 cup parmesan cheese), the egg, basil, salt and pepper. Stir together. Spread half of this mixture over the lasagna in the slow cooker.

Continue making another layer of noodles, then sauce, then cheese. Make a final layer of noodles, top with sauce, and sprinkle with the remaining 1/2 cup of parmesan cheese.

Cook on LOW for 4 hours.

Remove the insert from the slow cooker, and let it sit at room temperature for 10 minutes.

Serve warm.

South End Deep Root Chili {vegan}

Serves 8-10; can be halved, or doubled.

Black bean chili with a great backstory.

Ingredients

1-1/2 cups unsweetened apple juice
4 cups diced onion
1 cup diced celery
1 cup diced carrots
6 Tbsp minced garlic
4 tsp ground cumin
10 tsp chili powder, or to taste
4 cans black beans, drained, rinsed and drained again
28 oz vegetable stock (or chicken stock)
4 tsp lemon honey (or 4 tsp plain honey + 2 tsp fresh squeezed lemon or lime juice)
1 small dried chili pepper, crushed, or hot sauce to taste
1 28-oz can diced or chopped tomatoes, with juice
1/2 cup orzo (or other tiny pasta)
1/4 tsp salt (taste first if using storebought stock)
Black pepper to taste
Monterey Jack cheese, grated (for garnish)
Sour cream (for garnish)

Directions

Preheat a large heavy pot or Dutch oven on medium-high heat. Add apple juice and bring to a boil. Add onions and sauté, stirring, for 2 minutes. Add celery, carrots, garlic, cumin and chili powder. Continue stirring for 3 minutes. Add black beans, stock, honey, lemon, chili powder and tomatoes. Cover and bring to a boil, then reduce heat to low and simmer, covered, for 15 minutes, stirring occasionally to make sure the beans don't stick. Add orzo, salt and pepper, and continue cooking, covered, stirring frequently, until the orzo is cooked (8-10 minutes).

Serve hot, topped with Monterey Jack cheese and/or sour cream. Can be made ahead; cool, cover and refrigerate.

Spaghetti squash boat with clams, zucchini, peppers and olives {gluten-free}

Serves 2-4, depending on the size of your squash.

The most beautiful squash presentation!

Ingredients

1 small spaghetti squash
3 Tbsp extra virgin olive oil, divided
1 Tbsp capers, drained
1 tsp minced garlic
1 zucchini, seeded and diced
1/2 red bell pepper, seeded and diced
1/2 orange or yellow bell pepper, seeded and diced
1 6-oz can chopped clams, with their juice
2 Tbsp minced fresh basil (or basil from a tube)
1 small tomato, diced
2-3 Tbsp chopped, pitted kalamata olives
Juice of 1/2 lemon
2 Tbsp roughly chopped fresh flat-leaf parsley
Freshly ground black pepper, to taste
Grated Parmigiano-Reggiano cheese, 1/4 cup or more, to taste

Directions

Preheat oven to 400°F.

Carefully cut the squash in half lengthwise, and scoop out the seeds. [Note: if you have a microwave, cook the squash on high power for 5 minutes; this will make it much easier to cut.] Rub the squash inside and out with 1 tablespoon of olive oil, and place cut side down on a rimmed baking sheet. Cover with aluminum foil, and bake for 45 minutes, or until the rind is slightly soft and yields to the touch.

While the squash is baking, make the sauce.

Heat a sauté pan over medium-high heat, and add the remaining oil. Add the capers and garlic, and cook for 30 seconds, until the garlic is aromatic but not burned. Then, stir in the zucchini and bell peppers. Cook for 2 minutes, shaking the pan from time to time to keep things from sticking.

Pour in the clams, basil, tomato, olives and lemon juice. Let the sauce simmer for 5 minutes, until it reduces slightly. Add the fresh parsley, and black pepper to taste.

Fill each half of the squash with half of the vegetable mixture.

Top with plenty of grated cheese, and serve hot.

Spicy tuna and avocado ceviche

Serves 6-8 as an appetizer.

An exciting first course, for very hot days.

Ingredients

Juice of 1/2 lime
1 tsp sambal oelek
1 tsp reduced-sodium soy sauce
1/4 tsp kosher salt
1 large red or green scallion, minced
1 avocado, diced
1/2 lb *chilled* sushi-grade tuna, diced
2 tsp chopped fresh cilantro leaves

Directions

In a mixing bowl, combine lime juice, sambal, soy sauce and salt. Add remaining ingredients, and toss to coat.

The lime juice will begin to "cook" the fish, so make this at the last minute.

Serve immediately, while still cold, with crackers, toasted bread slices, or in lettuce leaves.

Steak sandwich with spicy harissa-lime sauce

Serves 4; can be multiplied.

A zippy sauce elevates this simple sandwich.

Ingredients

1/4 cup mayonnaise
1 tsp harissa paste, or more to taste
Juice of 1/2 lime
1/4 tsp fresh black pepper
Bread or rolls for 4 sandwiches
Lettuce leaves for 4 sandwiches
4-8 oz thinly sliced grilled steak, any cut (flank, skirt, sirloin, etc.), or store-bought roast beef

Directions

In a small bowl, whisk together the mayonnaise, harissa, lime juice and black pepper. Set aside.

Assemble the sandwiches: smear each top and bottom of the bread with sauce. On the bottom piece, layer some lettuce and steak.

Close the sandwiches, and serve.

Steamed baby bok choy with spicy hoisin glaze {vegan}

Figure on one or two heads per person, depending on what else is being served.

Look for baby bok choy at an Asian market.

Ingredients

1/2 cup hoisin sauce
1/4 cup low-sodium soy sauce
1-2 tsp Sriracha, to taste
1-2 tsp agave nectar or honey, to taste
Juice of half an orange or half a Meyer lemon
1-2 heads of baby bok choy per person

Directions

In a small glass measuring cup, whisk together the first five ingredients. The sauce should be viscous, like a glaze.

Prepare a steamer (bamboo, metal, whatever you have). Wash and rinse the bok choy and place it in the steam. Drizzle with a bit of the sauce. Cover the steamer, place over a pot filled with an inch of boiling water, and steam for 3-4 minutes, until the bok choy is just tender when pierced through the bulb with a sharp knife.

Remove bok choy from the steamer to a serving plate, and drizzle with a bit more of the sauce. You can save leftover sauce in a tightly-capped jar in the refrigerator. Serve hot.

Tapenade {vegan, gluten-free}

Makes 1 cup.

The easiest appetizer spread ever.

Ingredients

2 15-oz cans pitted black olives
1 16-oz jar green olives with red pimiento, whole or chopped
1 Tbsp capers
2 large cloves garlic, minced
3 Tbsp olive oil
Large pinch of kosher salt and black pepper, to taste

Directions

Couldn't be easier. Put everything in a food processor and pulse until olives are minced and all ingredients are combined. Add additional olive oil if desired to achieve a smoother texture.

Three mushroom risotto {gluten-free}

Serves 4 for main course, 6-8 for appetizer.

My favorite risotto, with lots of mushrooms.

Ingredients

6 cups chicken or beef broth (I use 4 cups of Swanson 99% fat free plus 2 cups of water, but homemade is great, if you have it)
1 cup water
2 oz dried porcini or any wild mushrooms
2-3 Tbsp olive oil
1/3 cup finely minced onion
2 cups arborio or carnaroli rice
1 cup white wine
14 oz fresh mushrooms (at least two types; I use cremini or baby bellas plus white button mushrooms), sliced
1 tsp chopped fresh thyme leaves
1 Tbsp tomato paste
2 Tbsp unsalted butter
1/3 cup Parmigiano-Reggiano cheese, grated, or more to taste
Black pepper (at least 1/2 tsp or more), to taste

Directions

Bring 6 cups of broth (or broth and water) to boil in a large pot and set aside at a simmer on the stove. In a microwave, boil 1 cup water in a glass measuring cup, then add dried mushrooms, and set aside. Heat oil in a large straight-sided sauté pan. Add onion, and sauté until soft. Stir in the rice, making sure to coat each grain, and let toast for 1-2 minutes.

Remove pan from heat, and stir in the wine (watch out for splatters). Keep stirring for a few seconds. When the liquid is absorbed, begin adding broth, 1 ladleful at a time, letting each bit of liquid be absorbed.

In the meantime, when the dried mushrooms are soft, strain and reserve the liquid. After 3 cups of broth are added, pour in the mushroom soaking water, being careful to leave behind the sediment in the bottom of the measuring cup. After 5 cups of broth are added, stir in the fresh mushrooms, thyme and tomato paste.

Continue adding one more cup of broth, reserving 1/4 cup. Stir until mushrooms have given off their liquid and almost all of the liquid in the pan has been absorbed by the rice.

Remove pan from heat. Add butter and cheese, and stir vigorously for 2 minutes. Add in reserved 1/4 cup broth, if needed to finish cooking the rice. Season to taste with lots of black pepper, and salt if needed, and serve immediately.

Tofu and Brussels sprouts fried rice {vegan}

Serves 4 as a main dish.

Use white or brown rice, and lots of veggies.

Ingredients

2 tsp peanut oil
1 clove garlic, minced
1/2 tsp minced (or grated) ginger root
1/4 cup chopped scallions
1/4 cup diced bell pepper (any color)
1 cup chopped mushrooms (any type; I like cremini)
1 cup trimmed and thinly sliced Brussels sprouts
1 cup drained extra-firm tofu, cut into 1/2-inch cubes
3 cups *cooked and cooled* white or brown rice
1 Tbsp sesame oil
1-2 Tbsp reduced-sodium soy sauce, to taste
Fresh black pepper, for garnish

Directions

Heat a wok or large frying pan over medium-high heat. When the pan is hot, pour in the peanut (or other neutral) oil.

Add the garlic and ginger, and stir for 15 seconds. Then, toss in the scallions, bell pepper, mushrooms and Brussels sprouts. Cook, stirring constantly, for 1-2 minutes, until the sprouts are bright green and tender.

Mix in the tofu, and stir-fry for 1 minute. Use your hands to break apart the cooled rice as you add it to the wok. Stir quickly, so the rice doesn't stick to the wok. Add the sesame oil, and stir quickly. Then, pour in the soy sauce. Keep stirring until all of the ingredients are incorporated.

Sprinkle with fresh black pepper (optional, but delicious). Serve hot.

Turkey, kale and cheese quesadillas

Serves 2; can be multiplied.

Dark leafy greens never tasted so good!

Ingredients

2 tsp olive oil
3 Tbsp chopped onion
4-5 cups chopped kale
2 Tbsp salsa or sofrito
2 large tortillas, any flavor
1/2 cup shredded cooked turkey
1/2 cup grated Cheddar cheese

Directions

In a large nonstick frying pan, heat the oil over low-medium heat. Sauté the onion for 2-3 minutes, until lightly browned. Add the kale and salsa or sofrito, and stir until the kale wilts and reduces in volume by half. Remove the pan from heat.

Preheat a griddle or a larger nonstick frying pan over medium heat.

Assemble the quesadillas: place the tortillas on your countertop. On one side of each of the tortillas, layer 2 Tbsp of cheese, half of the cooked kale, half of the chicken, and the rest of the cheese. Fold the tortilla in half, and place it on the griddle.

Cook until the tortilla is browned on the bottom, and the bottom layer of cheese has melted. With a spatula, gently flip the tortilla and cook until the second side is lightly browned.

Remove the quesadilla to a cutting board, and let it rest for 4-5 minutes before cutting into wedges with a serrated knife. Serve with additional salsa.

Turkey mole chili

The recipe serves 4-6, but you'll want to double it and freeze some.

Of all my chili variations, this one tops the list.

Ingredients

2 tsp canola or vegetable oil
1 lb ground turkey
1 large onion, diced
2 cloves garlic, minced
2 tsp chili powder (mild or hot, your favorite; I like Penzeys Chili 3000)
1 heaping tsp cumin
1/2 tsp sweet smoked paprika (pimenton dulce)
1/4 cup store-bought or homemade mole
1 12-oz bottle O'Doul's non-alcoholic beer or any beer you have on hand
1 15-oz can black beans, rinsed and drained
1 cup canned, chopped tomatoes
1-1/2 cups chicken stock
Kosher salt and fresh black pepper, to taste
Lime wedges, for serving

Directions

In a small Dutch oven, heat the oil. Add the turkey, and cook, stirring frequently, until the meat is no longer pink. Add the onion, and cook for 1 minute; then add the garlic, and cook for one minute more. Add the chili powder, cumin and smoked paprika, and stir for 30 seconds. Stir in the mole.

Pour in the beer, beans, tomato and chicken stock, and stir everything together. Reduce the heat to simmer, partially cover the pot, and cook for 30 minutes. Then uncover the pot and season to taste with salt and pepper.

Continue cooking, uncovered, for an additional 30 minutes, until the chili has thickened but there is still a bit of liquid in it. Serve over noodles, steamed rice, or on its own, garnished with a wedge of lime.

Turkey, red bean and cabbage soup {gluten-free}

Serves 10-12; can be doubled for a Soup Swap.

Bring this soup to a Soup Swap.

Ingredients

2 tsp olive oil
1 lb ground turkey (I use 93% fat-free)
1 large onion, diced
8 oz sliced mushrooms (cremini or white)
2 Tbsp fresh thyme leaves, or 1 Tbsp dried thyme leaf
2 Tbsp Dijon mustard
10 cups chicken stock, homemade or low-sodium store-bought (gluten-free if needed)
2 cups kidney beans, cooked, or 4 cups canned kidney beans (drained and rinsed)
14-oz bag coleslaw mix, or 14 oz shredded green cabbage
2 Tbsp white balsamic vinegar
2 Tbsp agave nectar
1/4 cup roughly chopped fresh flat-leaf parsley
1 tsp fresh black pepper
Kosher salt, to taste

Directions

In a very large stock pot, heat the olive oil over medium heat. Sauté the turkey in the oil until the meat is no longer pink, and use a wooden spoon to break up any large clumps. Stir in the onion, and cook until translucent, 2-3 minutes. Add the mushrooms, thyme, and Dijon mustard, and give a swirl or two. Pour in the chicken stock. Raise heat to high, and when the stock is warm (not yet boiling), add the beans and cole slaw mix. Stir for a few minutes, until the cabbage wilts. Season the soup with white balsamic vinegar and agave. Then reduce heat to simmer, and cook uncovered for 45 minutes. When the soup has reduced slightly, sprinkle in the parsley and black pepper. If you've used homemade stock, you might need to add as much as a teaspoon of kosher salt, or whatever tastes good to you. Some of the beans will have opened, and thickened the soup a bit. If you'd like, use the back of your wooden spoon to encourage a few more beans to open. Serve hot. Can be made ahead, cooled and refrigerated, or frozen in airtight containers.

Vegetable fried (brown) rice

Serves 1; can be multiplied.

Brown rice adds nutty flavor to this recipe.

Ingredients

2 tsp peanut, vegetable or rice bran oil
1 egg, lightly scrambled
1 cup diced mixed vegetables -- onion, bell pepper, Napa cabbage, etc.
1 cup broccoli florets, blanched for 1 minute in boiling water (or steamed in a microwave)
1 cup *cooked* brown rice, chilled
1 tsp oyster sauce (omit for vegetarian, and use 2 tsp soy sauce)
1 tsp reduced-sodium soy sauce
Salt and pepper to taste (a pinch of each)
1/2 tsp sesame oil

Directions

Heat the oil in a wok over highest heat, and add the egg. Stir quickly!

Immediately add the vegetables, and continue to stir for 15 seconds.

Add rice, oyster sauce, soy sauce, and salt and pepper, and stir for 1 minute; the sauce should be absorbed and the rice grains should be separate.

Add the sesame oil, toss, and serve hot.

West African chicken mafé (chicken stew in peanut sauce) {gluten-free}

Serves 6-8.

A beautiful stew for entertaining.

Ingredients

2-1/2 lb boneless, skinless chicken thighs, trimmed and cut into 1-inch pieces
1-1/2 lb boneless, skinless chicken breasts, trimmed and cut into 1-inch pieces
1 tsp kosher salt
1 tsp ground black pepper
3 tsp chopped garlic, divided
1/2 to 1 tsp ground cayenne pepper (use lesser amount for a bit less heat)
2 tbsp vegetable oil
1 small yellow onion, finely diced
1 small red bell pepper, seeded and finely diced
1/2 green bell pepper, seeded and finely diced
1 small jalapeño pepper, seeds and ribs removed, finely diced
4 cups chicken broth, low-sodium store-bought or homemade
1/2 cup smooth peanut butter
1 Tbsp tomato paste
1/4 cup drained canned chopped tomato
1/2 tsp dried thyme
1 tsp peeled, grated fresh ginger root
1/2 cup coconut milk
1/4 cup chopped cilantro or parsley, for garnish

Directions

Place the chicken pieces in a large mixing bowl, and add the salt, black pepper, 2 teaspoons of chopped garlic, and cayenne. Use your hands to mix everything together, making sure the spices are distributed all over the chicken.

Wash your hands well.

Heat the oil in a large nonstick frying pan over medium high heat. Add the chicken, in batches if necessary to avoid overcrowding the pan, and brown on all sides, then transfer to a platter or bowl.

To the oil remaining in the pan, add the onion, bell peppers, the remaining garlic, and jalapeño. Sauté the vegetables for 4-5 minutes until soft.

Pour in the chicken broth and simmer for 20 minutes, uncovered. Reduce the heat to medium-low, and stir in the peanut butter, tomato paste, canned tomato, thyme, ginger and coconut milk, and simmer for two minutes, whisking to incorporate the ingredients. Return the browned chicken to the pan and cook uncovered over low heat 30-40 minutes, stirring occasionally, until the chicken is tender and the sauce thickens.

Garnish with chopped cilantro or parsley, and serve hot, over rice.

West African vegetable stew in peanut sauce {vegan, gluten-free}

Serves 4-6.

A knockout vegan dish for entertaining.

Ingredients

1 medium onion, quartered
2 large red-skinned new potatoes, cut into 1-inch chunks
2 zucchini, cut into 1-inch chunks
2 bell peppers, cut into 1-inch chunks (use any colors)
1 tsp kosher salt
1 tsp ground black pepper
2 large garlic cloves, minced
1/4 tsp cayenne pepper
2 tbsp olive oil
1 small jalapeño pepper, seeds and ribs removed, minced
8 oz sliced mushrooms, any type (I like cremini)
1 15-oz can chickpeas, drained and rinsed
1/2 cup smooth peanut butter
1 Tbsp harissa
1/4 cup drained canned chopped tomato
1 tsp peeled, grated fresh ginger root
1/2 cup coconut milk
1/4 cup chopped parsley, for garnish

Directions

Place the onion, potatoes, zucchini and bell peppers in a large mixing bowl, and add the salt, black pepper, chopped garlic, and cayenne. Use your hands to mix everything together, making sure the spices are distributed all over the vegetables.

Heat the olive oil in a large nonstick frying pan over medium heat. Add the vegetables from the mixing bowl, all at once. Sauté 4-5 minutes, until the onions are translucent and there are bits of browning on the vegetables.

Add the jalapeño pepper and mushrooms, and continue to cook, stirring occasionally, for 3 minutes. Then, stir in the chickpeas, peanut butter, harissa, chopped tomatoes, ginger, and coconut milk.

Add 2 cups of water. Bring to a simmer, and cook uncovered, stirring occasionally, for 25-30 minutes, or until the sauce thickens.

Garnish with chopped parsley, and serve hot, over rice.

Zucchini waffles {vegetarian}

Makes 8 waffles.

Kids won't know there's zucchini hiding inside.

Ingredients

2 medium zucchini, ends trimmed
1-1/2 cups all-purpose unbleached flour
1 Tbsp baking powder
1 tsp kosher salt
1 tsp cinnamon
1/3 cup sugar
1-1/2 cups skim (nonfat) milk
2 large eggs
1 tsp pure vanilla extract
Cooking spray

Directions

Grate the zucchini on the large holes of a box grater. Place in a strainer, and sprinkle with a teaspoon or so of kosher salt. Place the strainer over a bowl, and let the zucchini drain for 30 minutes. Rinse under cold water, shake off excess liquid, and transfer the zucchini to a clean dish towel. Squeeze out as much moisture as you can from the zucchini, and set aside.

Preheat waffle maker to 400°F.

In a large mixing bowl, combine flour, baking powder, salt, cinnamon and sugar. Stir together.

In another large bowl, whisk together the milk, eggs, and vanilla extract. Add the dry ingredients (the flour mixture), and beat until smooth. Stir in the zucchini and mix well.

Spray the waffle maker with cooking spray (top and bottom plates). Spread half of the batter evenly over the bottom of the waffle maker, and close the top. Cook for 5 minutes, or until the waffles are as crisp as you like them. (Different waffle making equipment will cook at different rates, so please follow the instructions that come with your machine.) Repeat with remaining batter.

Serve hot, topped with sweet butter and maple syrup.

Where to find a zillion more recipes from The Perfect Pantry

On the blog:

www.theperfectpantry.com

In my ebooks

(readable on ANY device with the free Kindle reading app):

23 Zucchini: Fast, fun, easy recipes

25 Tomatoes: Easy year-round recipes using fresh, canned, roasted, and sun-dried tomatoes

Meatballs: Low-fat turkey meatball recipes with bold around-the-world flavors

Dress Up Your Salad: Turn everyday ingredients into exciting salads

Meatless Holidays: Fun, festive recipes for vegetarians, vegans, and the people who cook for them

See all of my books on my Amazon author page:

www.amazon.com/author/lydiawalshin